Quiz Champs
Human Body Systems

Manisha Nayak

WS Education

NEW JERSEY • LONDON • SINGAPORE • BEIJING • SHANGHAI • HONG KONG • TAIPEI • CHENNAI • TOKYO

Published by

WS Education, an imprint of
World Scientific Publishing Co. Pte. Ltd.
5 Toh Tuck Link, Singapore 596224
USA office: 27 Warren Street, Suite 401-402, Hackensack, NJ 07601
UK office: 57 Shelton Street, Covent Garden, London WC2H 9HE

National Library Board, Singapore Cataloguing in Publication Data
Name(s): Nayak, Manisha.
Title: Human body systems / Manisha Nayak.
Other Title(s): Quiz champs.
Description: Singapore : WS Education, [2024]
Identifier(s): ISBN 978-981-12-7460-2 (hardback) | 978-981-12-7491-6 (paperback) |
 978-981-12-7461-9 (ebook for institutions) | 978-981-12-7462-6 (ebook for individuals)
Subject(s): LCSH: Human physiology--Juvenile literature. | Human body-Juvenile literature.
Classification: DDC 612--dc23

British Library Cataloguing-in-Publication Data
A catalogue record for this book is available from the British Library.

All photos from Shutterstock.com.

Copyright © 2024 by World Scientific Publishing Co. Pte. Ltd.

All rights reserved. This book, or parts thereof, may not be reproduced in any form or by any means, electronic or mechanical, including photocopying, recording or any information storage and retrieval system now known or to be invented, without written permission from the publisher.

For photocopying of material in this volume, please pay a copying fee through the Copyright Clearance Center, Inc., 222 Rosewood Drive, Danvers, MA 01923, USA. In this case permission to photocopy is not required from the publisher.

Design and layout by Rosie Gowsell Pattison/Plan B Book Packagers

Desk editor: Daniele Lee

Printed in Singapore

Welcome to the wonderful World of Science!

How to use this book

- Read the questions on the following pages and try to guess the correct answers.

- You can start at the beginning of the book or do the quizzes in any order.

- Do the quizzes by yourself or with a friend or family member.

- Keep score to see how many answers you get right.

- At the end of the book, you'll find a bonus quiz where you can match keywords to their meanings.

- You'll also find a bonus crossword puzzle, which you can use to decipher a password to unlock a special *Quiz Champs* certificate!

Find me, your Quiz Champs host, hidden in 25 pictures in this book. (Answers on page 167.)

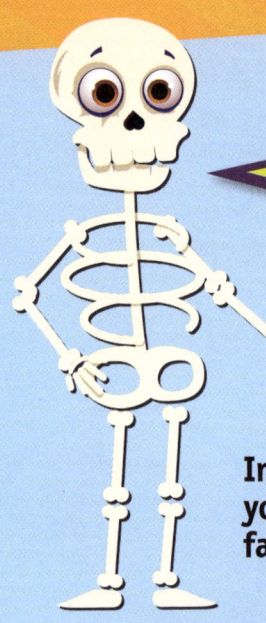

Hi! I'm Skip, part-time skeleton and part-time quizmaster!

In this edition of *Quiz Champs*, you'll test your knowledge and learn more about some fascinating human body systems!

You'll also find:

Jokes and riddles to make you giggle

Heehee!

Did You Know?
Boxes filled with fun and unusual facts about the human body

The human body is a very complex machine. It is made of many different systems, such as the digestive system and the circulatory system. A system is made of different parts, and each part has a function. The various parts work together to make the system work properly.

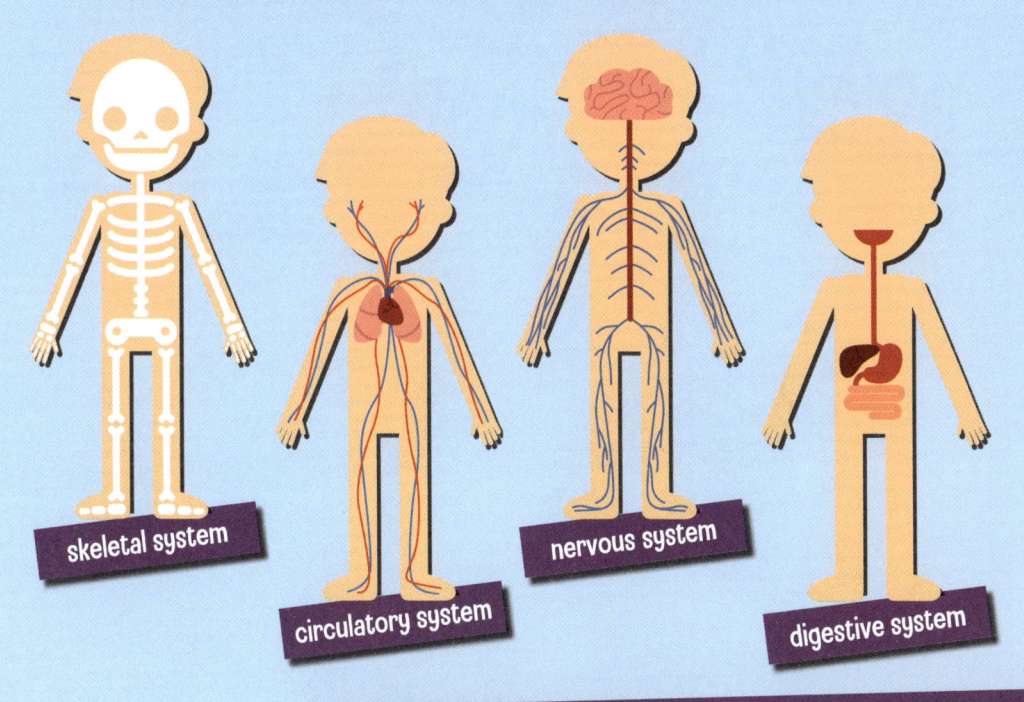

skeletal system

circulatory system

nervous system

digestive system

Ready to see how much you know about human body systems? Turn the page and let's go!

Which of these body parts is NOT a sense organ?

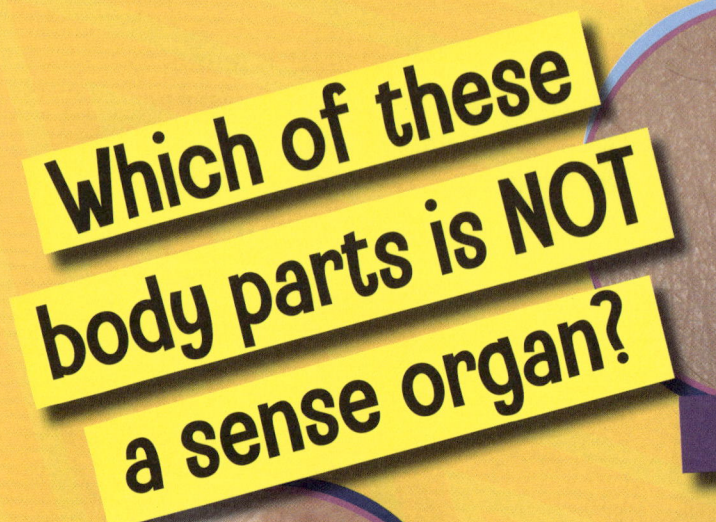

skin

eye

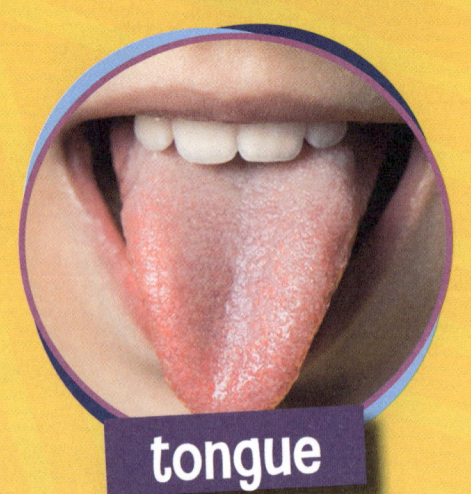

tongue

nose

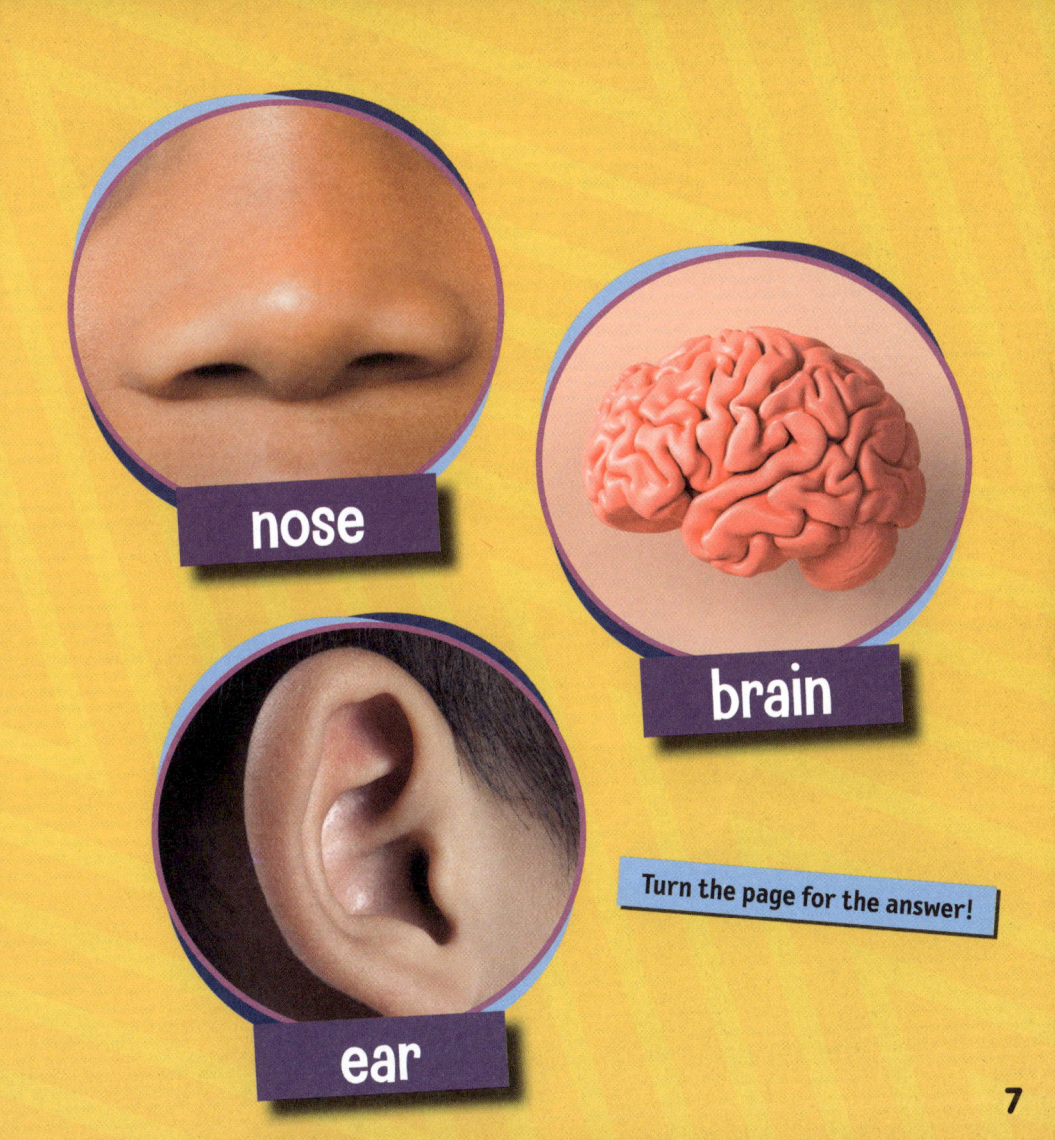

brain

ear

Turn the page for the answer!

7

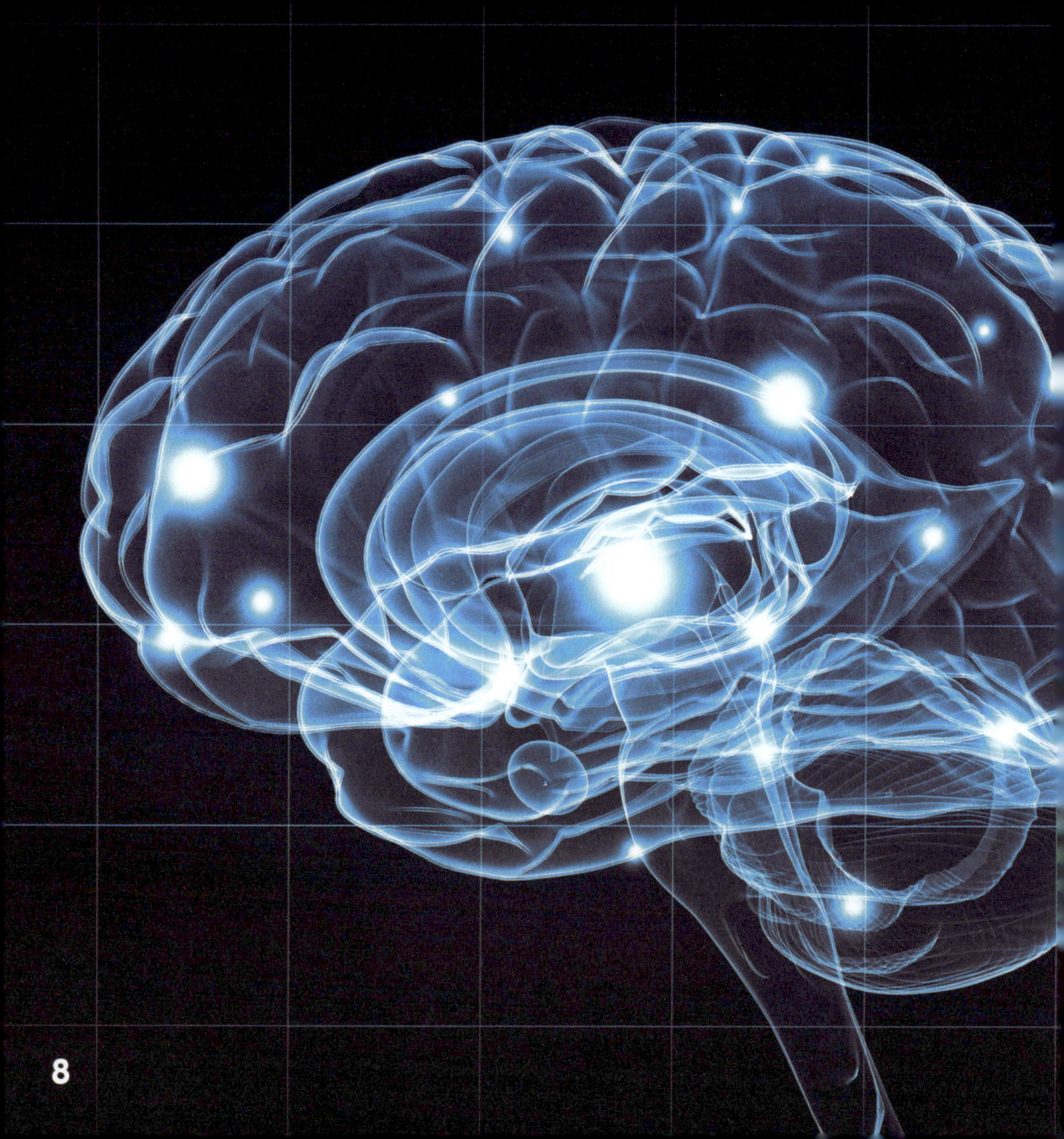

ANSWER:

The brain is not a sense organ.

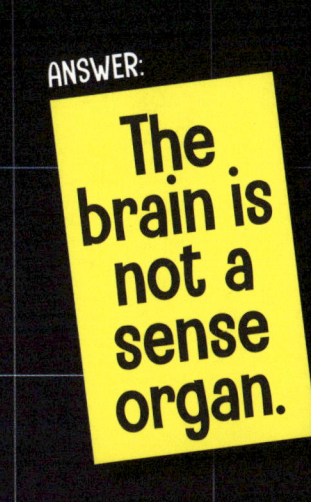

An organ is a part of the body that carries out a specific function. We have five sense organs that help us collect information about things around us. Our sense organs are the eyes, nose, ears, skin and tongue. The brain is not a sense organ, but it uses the information collected by the sense organs to tell us what to do.

What kind of advice did the ear give the eye?

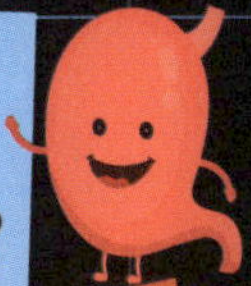

Sound advice!

Did You Know?

Each sense organ is associated with a particular sense.

SENSE ORGAN	SENSE
eyes	sight
nose	smell
ears	hearing
skin	touch
tongue	taste

What is the human body's largest organ?

ANSWER: Skin.

The skin is the largest organ of the body. The total area of skin in an average adult is about 2 square metres. The skin has many functions, but its main job is to act as a barrier that protects the inside of the body from external factors such as injuries and germs.

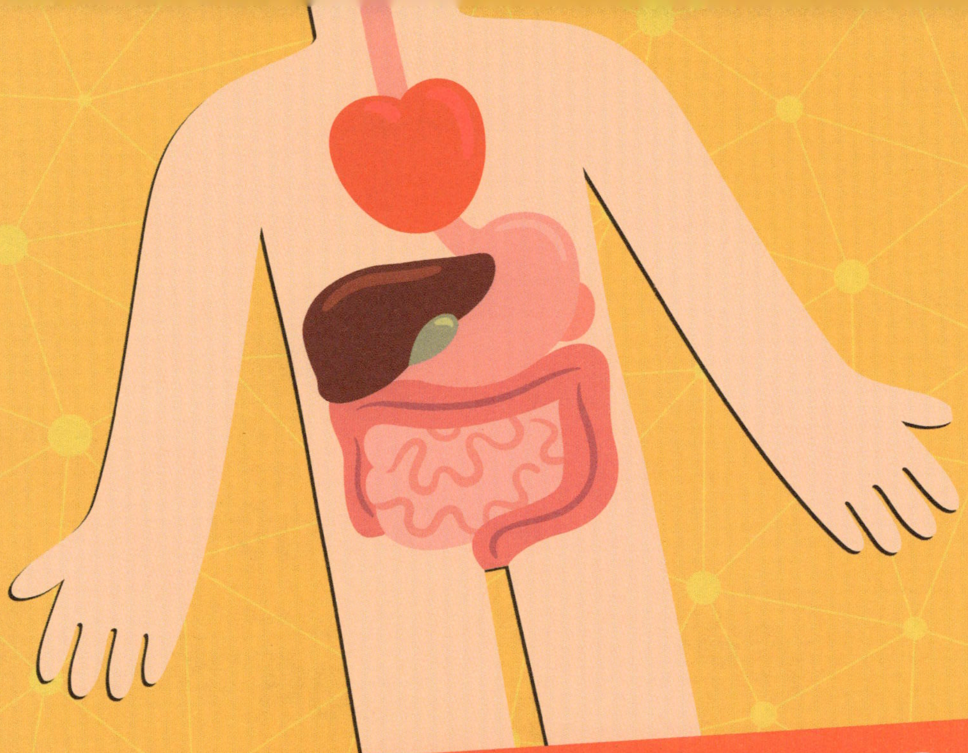

Did You Know?

The skin is an external organ, which means that it is found outside the body. Internal organs are found inside the body. The largest internal organ in the human body is the liver.

What body system is made up of bones?

12

Why was the skeleton lonely?

Because it had no body to talk to!

ANSWER:

The skeletal system.

Your skeletal system is made up of bones. It supports your body and gives it shape. It works with your muscles to help you move. It also protects delicate organs, such as your heart and lungs.

TRUE or FALSE?

A baby has more bones than an adult.

ANSWER: True!

An adult has 206 bones. A baby has about 300 bones at birth. Many of the bones fuse together as the baby grows, to eventually form the 206 bones.

What do bones say before leaving on vacation?

Bone voyage!

15

TRUE or FALSE?

Why are giraffes so popular?

Because everyone looks up to them!

Giraffes and humans have the same number of neck bones.

ANSWER: True!

A giraffe may have a very long neck, but it has seven bones in its neck—the same as a human! The neck bones in giraffes are longer than the neck bones in humans.

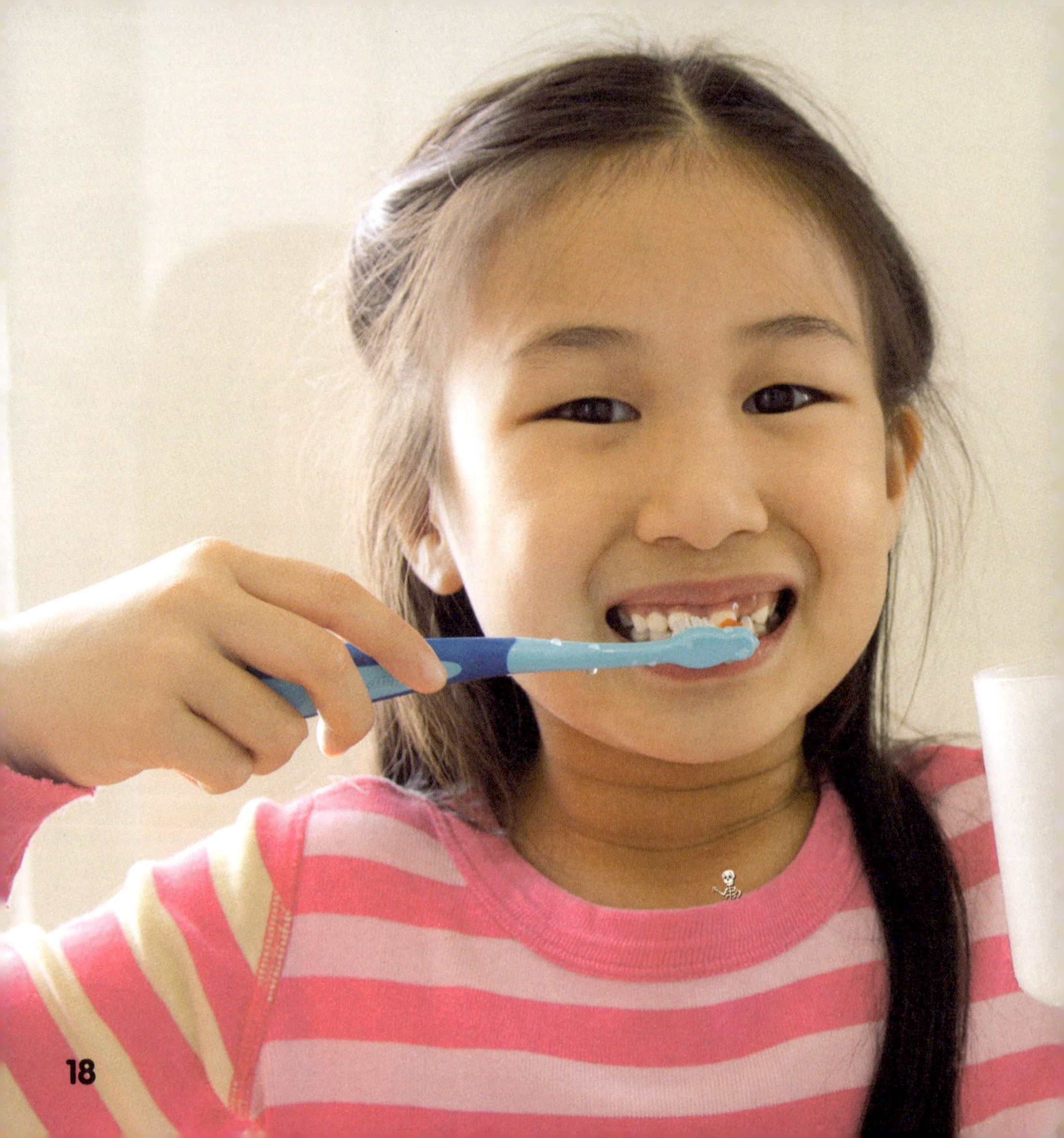

How many baby teeth do humans have?

ANSWER: Twenty! Most babies are born without any teeth. They grow their first set of 20 teeth, commonly known as baby teeth. Baby teeth usually fall out between the ages of 6 and 12. They are replaced by a set of 32 adult teeth.

Which part of your body has the longest bone?

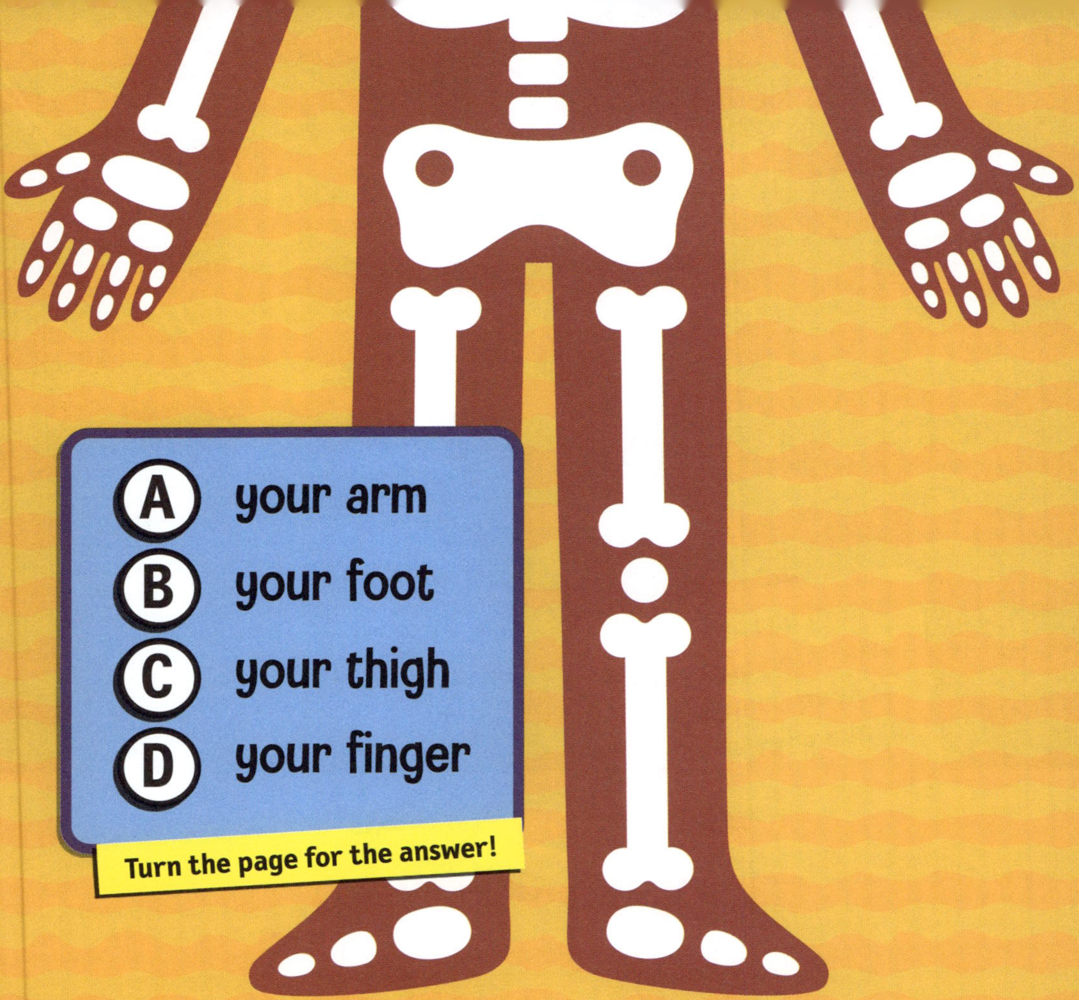

- A your arm
- B your foot
- C your thigh
- D your finger

Turn the page for the answer!

ANSWER: C

your thigh

The longest bone in the human body is the thigh bone, also known as the femur.

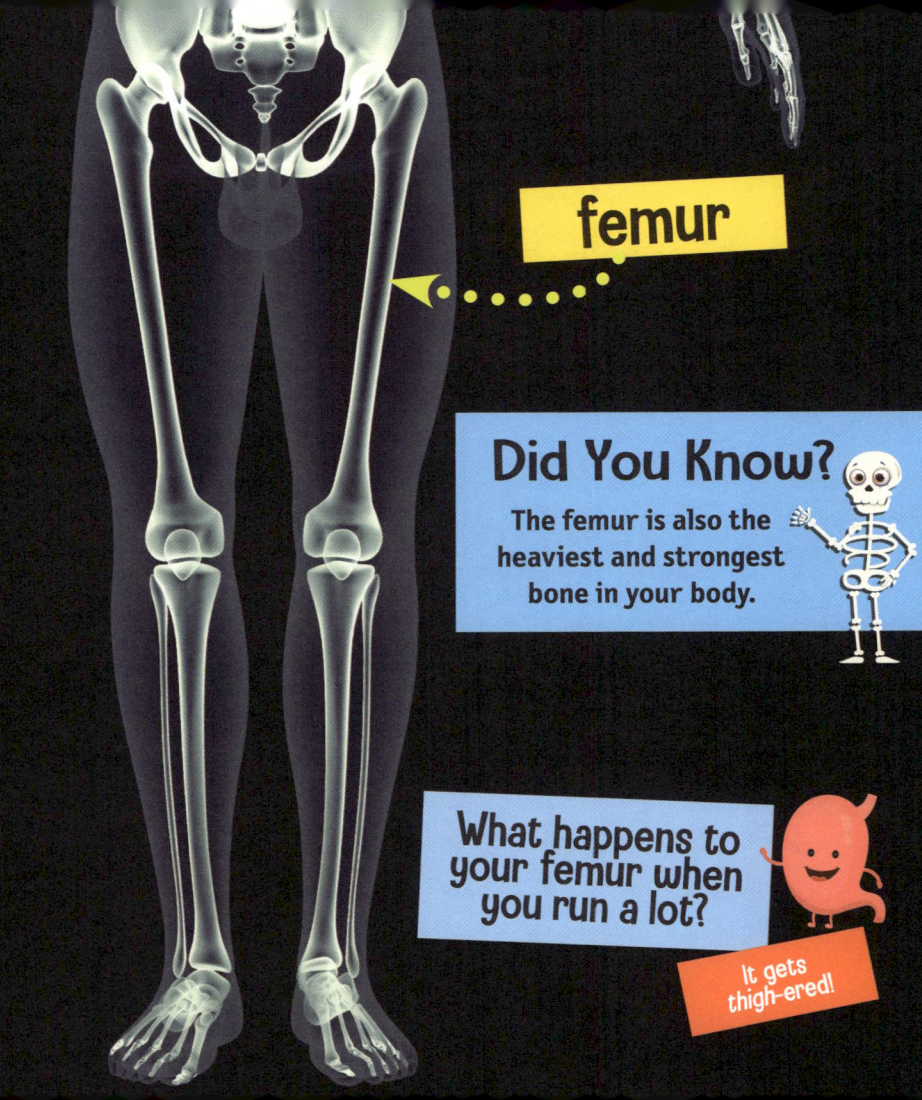

femur

Did You Know?

The femur is also the heaviest and strongest bone in your body.

What happens to your femur when you run a lot?

It gets thigh-ered!

23

Which part of your skeletal system protects your heart?

- **A)** your skull
- **B)** your femur
- **C)** your ribcage
- **D)** your backbone

Turn the page for the answer!

25

ANSWER: **C**

your ribcage

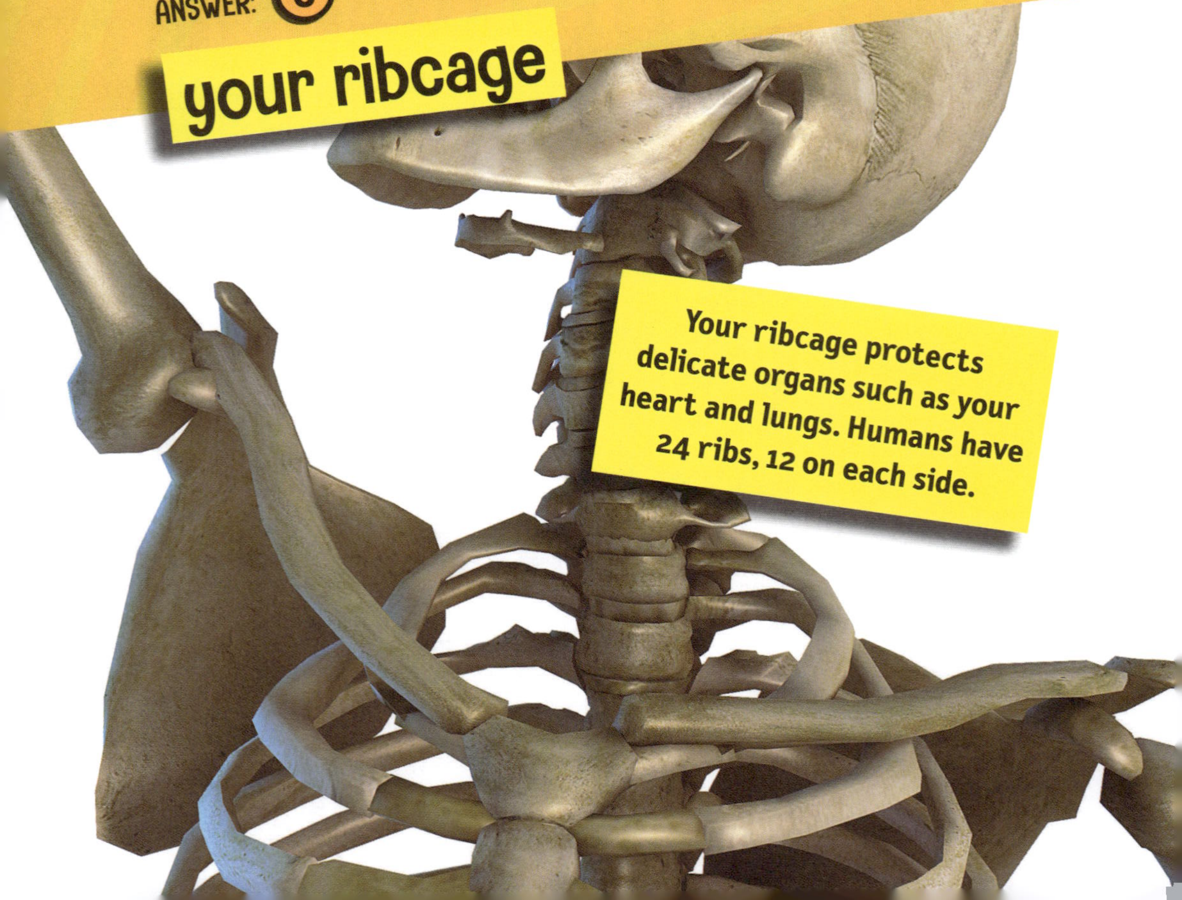

Your ribcage protects delicate organs such as your heart and lungs. Humans have 24 ribs, 12 on each side.

Where do you keep a bird skeleton?

Inside a ribcage!

27

TRUE or FALSE?

Broken bones can repair themselves.

ANSWER: True!

Bones have the amazing ability to repair and rebuild themselves. Depending on the type of broken bone (also known as a fracture), it may take several weeks to several months. A cast is used to hold the broken bones in place until they heal.

What do you call a cast after it is removed?

A cast-away!

Which is harder—your bones or your teeth?

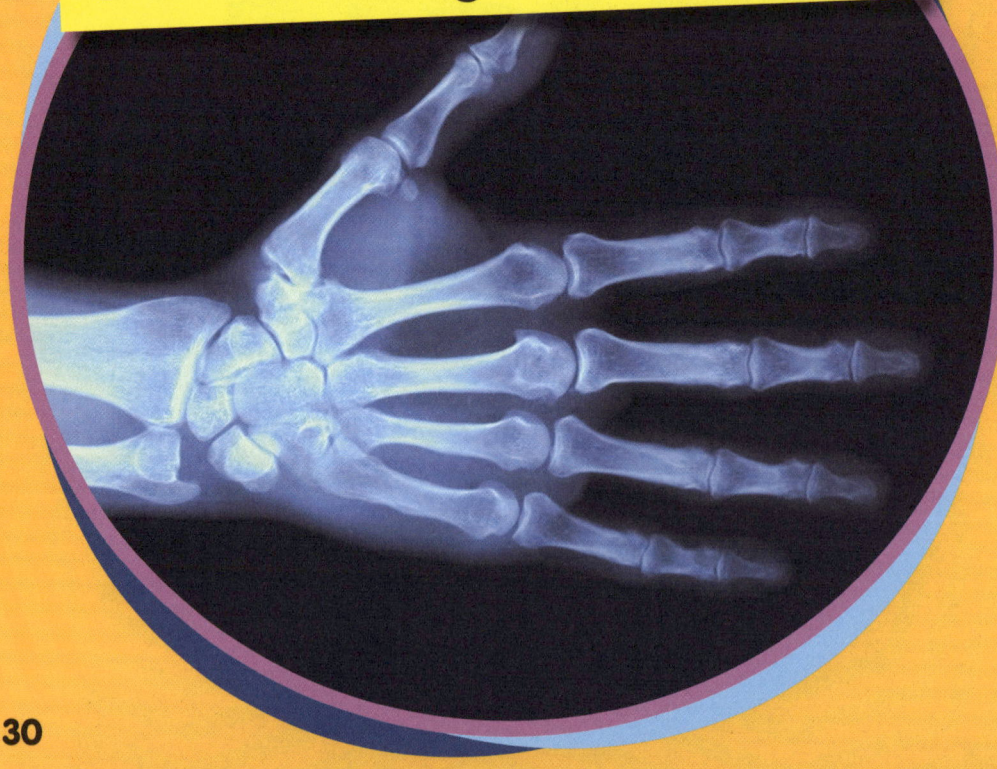

ANSWER: Your teeth.

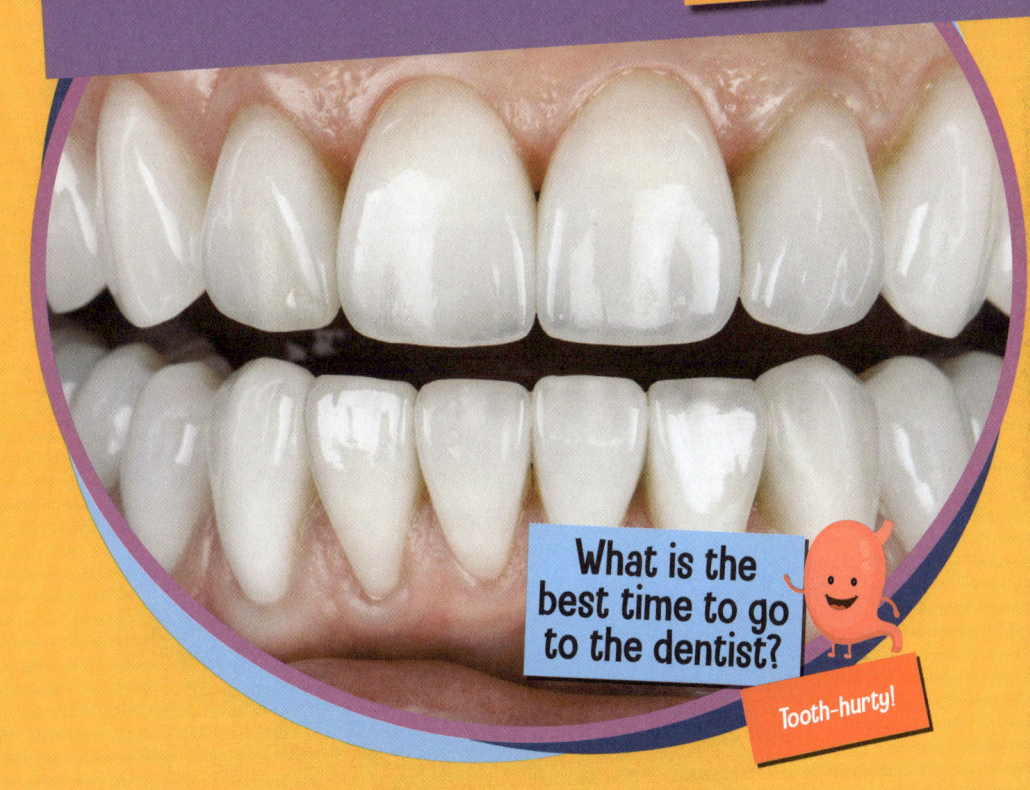

Your teeth are covered in a substance called enamel, which is the white, visible part of your teeth. Enamel is the hardest substance in your body. It protects your teeth from damage. However, consuming too much of fizzy drinks and acidic food can damage the enamel.

What is the best time to go to the dentist?

Tooth-hurty!

What is the name of this muscle?

ANSWER: Biceps.

Different muscles make up your muscular system. Your muscles work with your bones to allow you to move your body in different ways. Your biceps allow you to bend your elbows and do things like catch and throw a ball.

Which sea animals can you find in the gym?

Mussels!

Did You Know?
The word 'muscle' comes from the Latin word 'musculus', which means 'little mouse'. This is because flexed biceps were thought to resemble a little mouse.

TRUE or FALSE?

We control all the muscles in our body.

ANSWER: False!

Not all muscles in our body are controlled by us. For example, muscles in the heart work automatically without us controlling them.

35

Which muscles work throughout your life without resting?

- A muscles in the legs
- B muscles in the face
- C muscles in the arms
- D muscles in the heart

ANSWER: Ⓓ muscles in the heart
The muscles in the heart, known as the cardiac muscles, work continuously on their own throughout our lives.

37

TRUE or FALSE?

Exercising makes our bones and muscles stronger.

38

ANSWER: **True!**

Exercise is very important to keep your body strong and healthy. Exercise makes your muscles bigger and stronger. Stronger muscles pull harder on the bones, and as a result, the bones become stronger too.

Why did the bicycle stop exercising?

It was two-tyred!

39

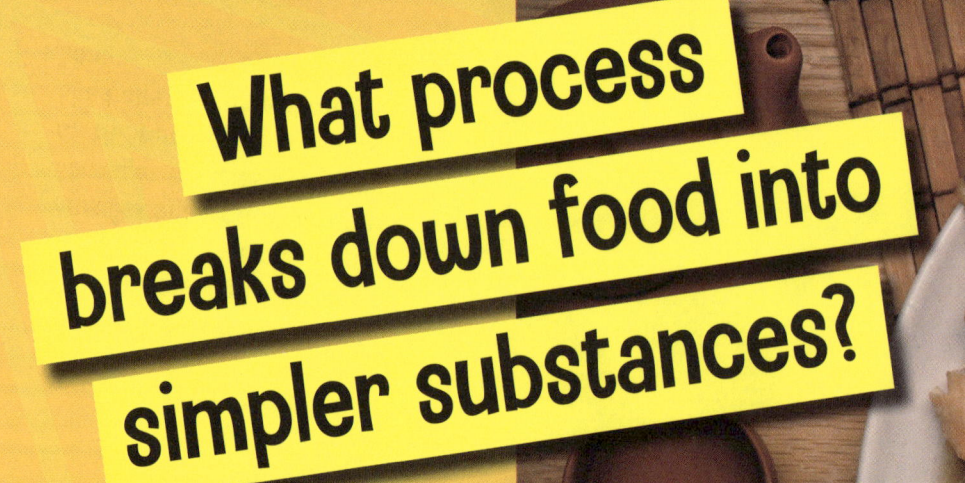

What process breaks down food into simpler substances?

- **A** chewing
- **B** digestion
- **C** absorption
- **D** swallowing

Turn the page for the answer!

40

41

ANSWER: **B** **digestion**

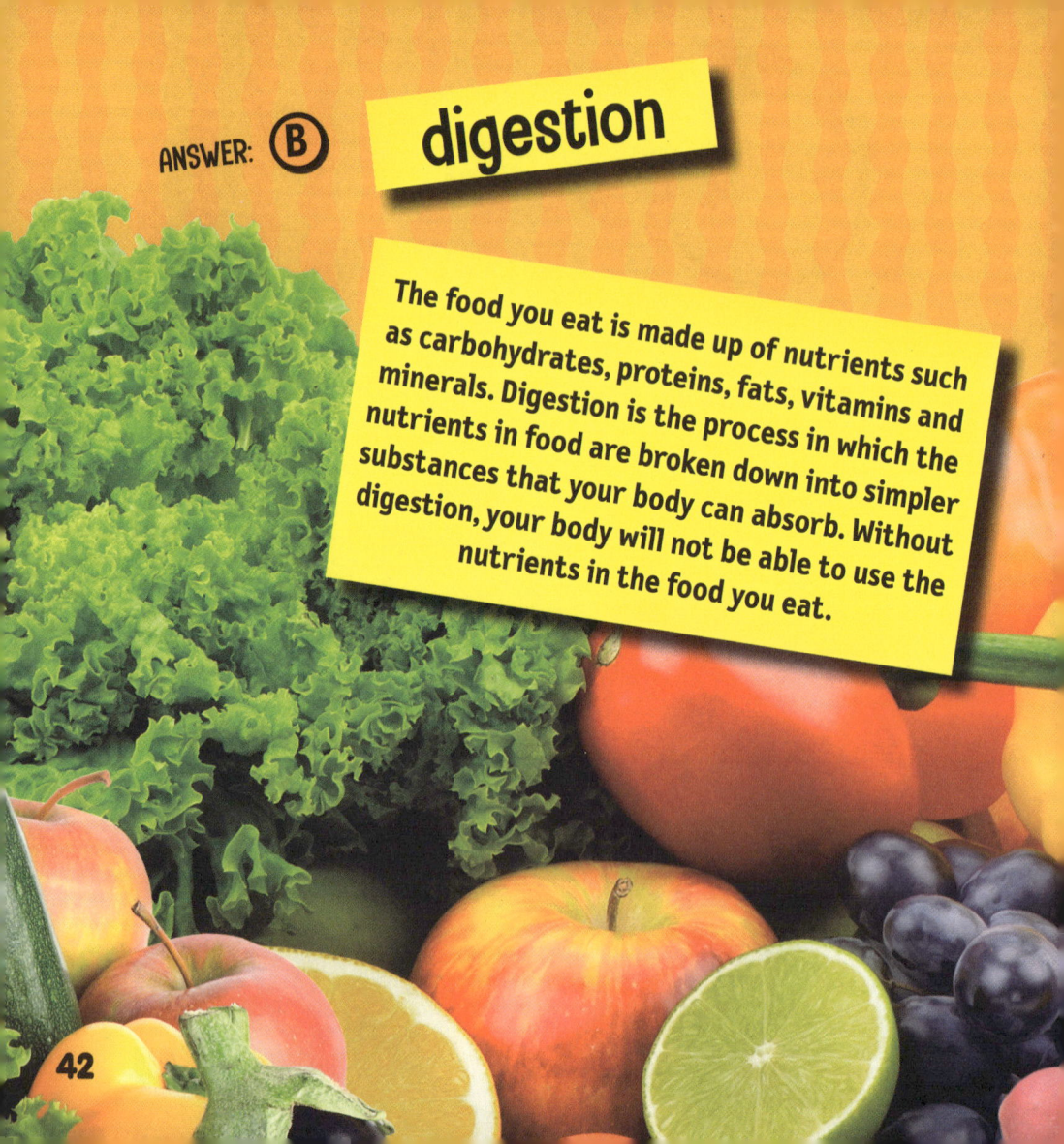

The food you eat is made up of nutrients such as carbohydrates, proteins, fats, vitamins and minerals. Digestion is the process in which the nutrients in food are broken down into simpler substances that your body can absorb. Without digestion, your body will not be able to use the nutrients in the food you eat.

Did You Know?

Digestion starts the moment you put food in your mouth. Your saliva contains substances called digestive juices that start the process of digestion.

How much saliva do we produce in a day?

ANSWER: 0.5 to 1.5 litres.

Saliva is produced by special organs in the mouth, called salivary glands. Saliva has several functions. It moistens food to help us swallow it easily and also contains digestive juices that help to break down food into simpler substances that your body can absorb.

Did You Know?
Ever wondered why the sight of your favourite food makes your mouth water? When you see, smell or even think about food you like, your brain sends signals to your mouth to produce more saliva to prepare for digestion!

45

How is chewing food helpful?

ANSWER: It makes digestion easier and faster.

Chewing food helps to break it into smaller pieces. This makes it easier for us to swallow the food. Chewing also exposes a larger surface area of the food to digestive juices, which makes digestion faster and easier.

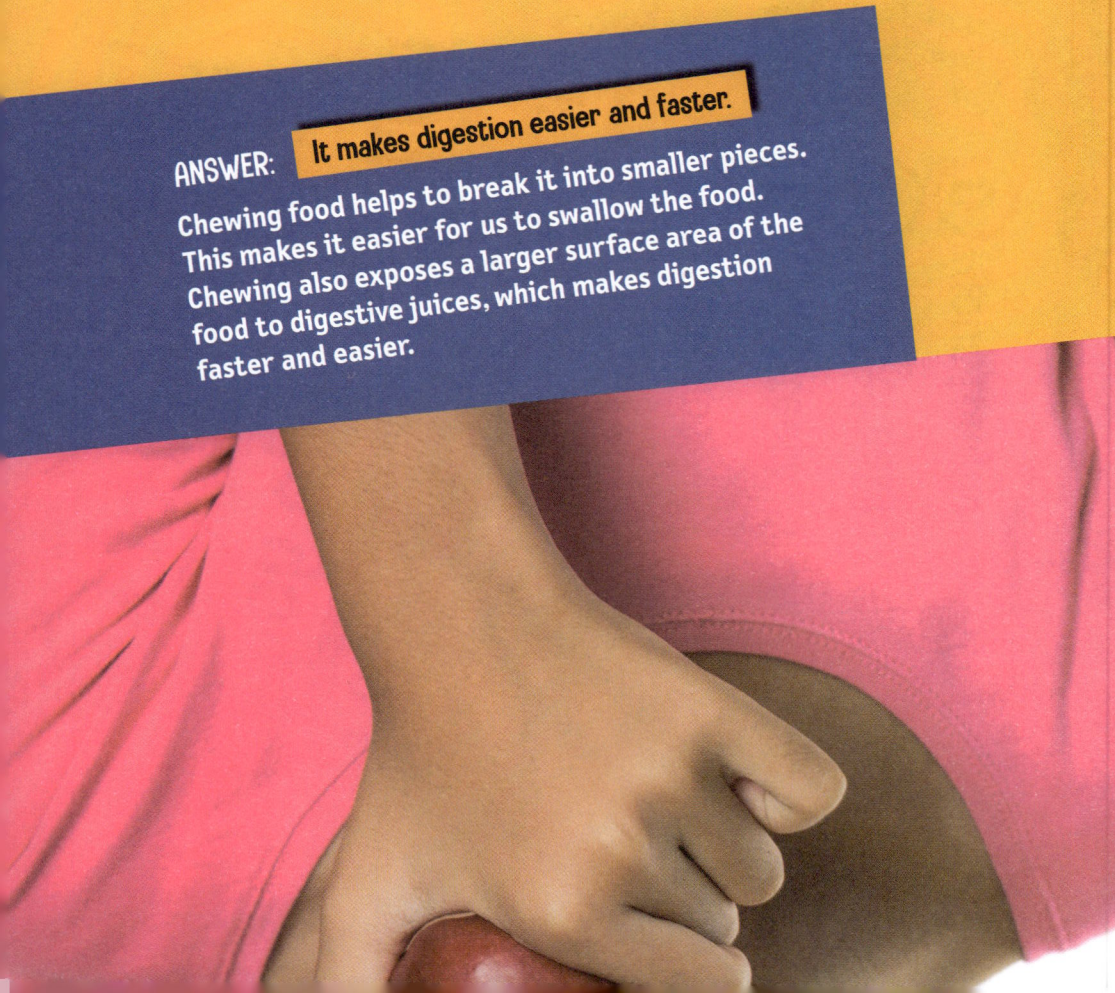

47

Which part of your body do you use to taste food?

- **A** your lips
- **B** your teeth
- **C** your cheeks
- **D** your tongue

ANSWER: ⓓ your tongue

The surface of your tongue has bumps that contain sensory organs called taste buds. Taste buds allow you to experience tastes, such as sweet, salty, sour and bitter.

Did You Know?

In addition to the four basic tastes, scientists have also discovered a fifth taste called 'umami'. Japanese for 'pleasant, savoury taste', umami is used to describe food that has a brothy or meaty taste. Some examples of food with umami taste are cheese, seaweed and mushrooms.

49

What is the oesophagus also known as?

oesophagus

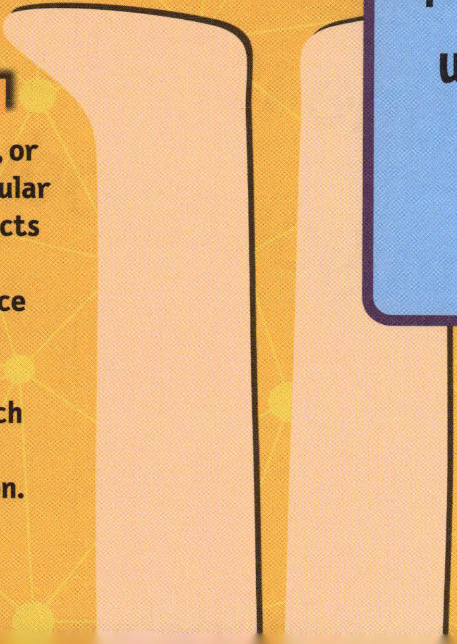

ANSWER:
Ⓑ the gullet

The oesophagus, or gullet, is a muscular tube that connects the mouth and the stomach. Once swallowed, food travels through this tube to reach the stomach for further digestion.

- Ⓐ the anus
- Ⓑ the gullet
- Ⓒ the rectum
- Ⓓ the stomach

Did You Know?

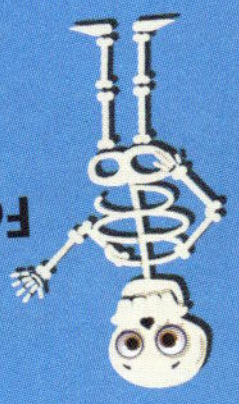

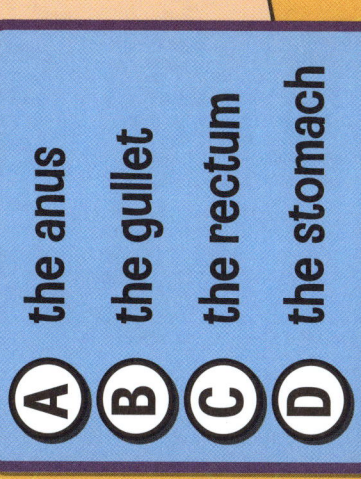

Food can move along your digestive system even if you're upside down! Food moves along your digestive system not because of gravity, but because of the wave-like movement of the muscles in the digestive system.

TRUE or FALSE?

Your small intestine is longer than your body.

ANSWER: True!

The small intestine is a part of your digestive system. Digested food is absorbed by the walls of the small intestine into your bloodstream. Your small intestine is about 5 metres long. It is folded over many times to fit into your abdomen. However, if stretched out, it is much longer than your body!

In which of these organs are NO digestive juices released?

A. the mouth
B. the stomach
C. the small intestine
D. the large intestine

ANSWER:
Ⓓ the large intestine

The main function of the large intestine is to absorb water from undigested food before it is removed from the body as waste.

Did You Know?

The large intestine is so named due to its width, not its length. It is wider and shorter than the small intestine.

What is the name of this organ?

ANSWER: The liver. The liver has many functions. It produces a digestive juice called bile, removes harmful substances known as toxins from your blood, and stores energy in the form of a sugar called glycogen.

Did You Know?

The liver is the only organ in the body that can regenerate itself. Even if there is only a quarter of the liver intact, it can regrow to its original size.

Which system transports digested food to all parts of the body?

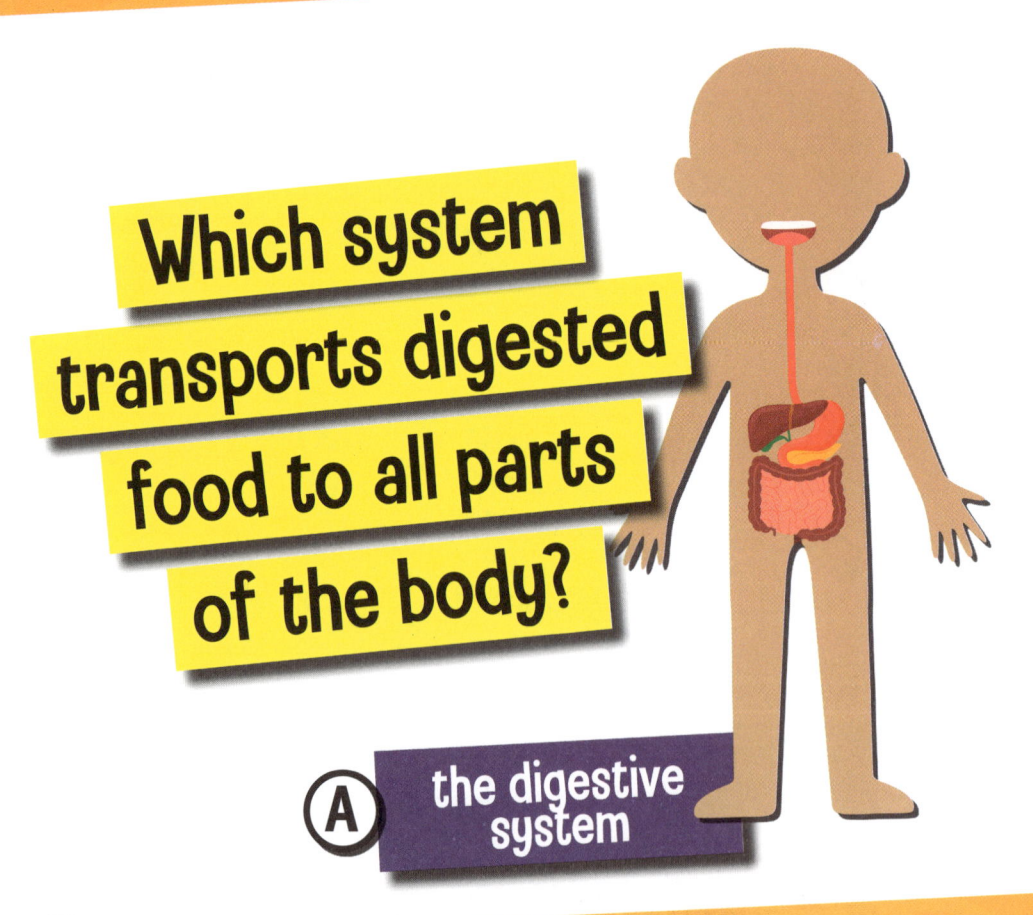

A the digestive system

58

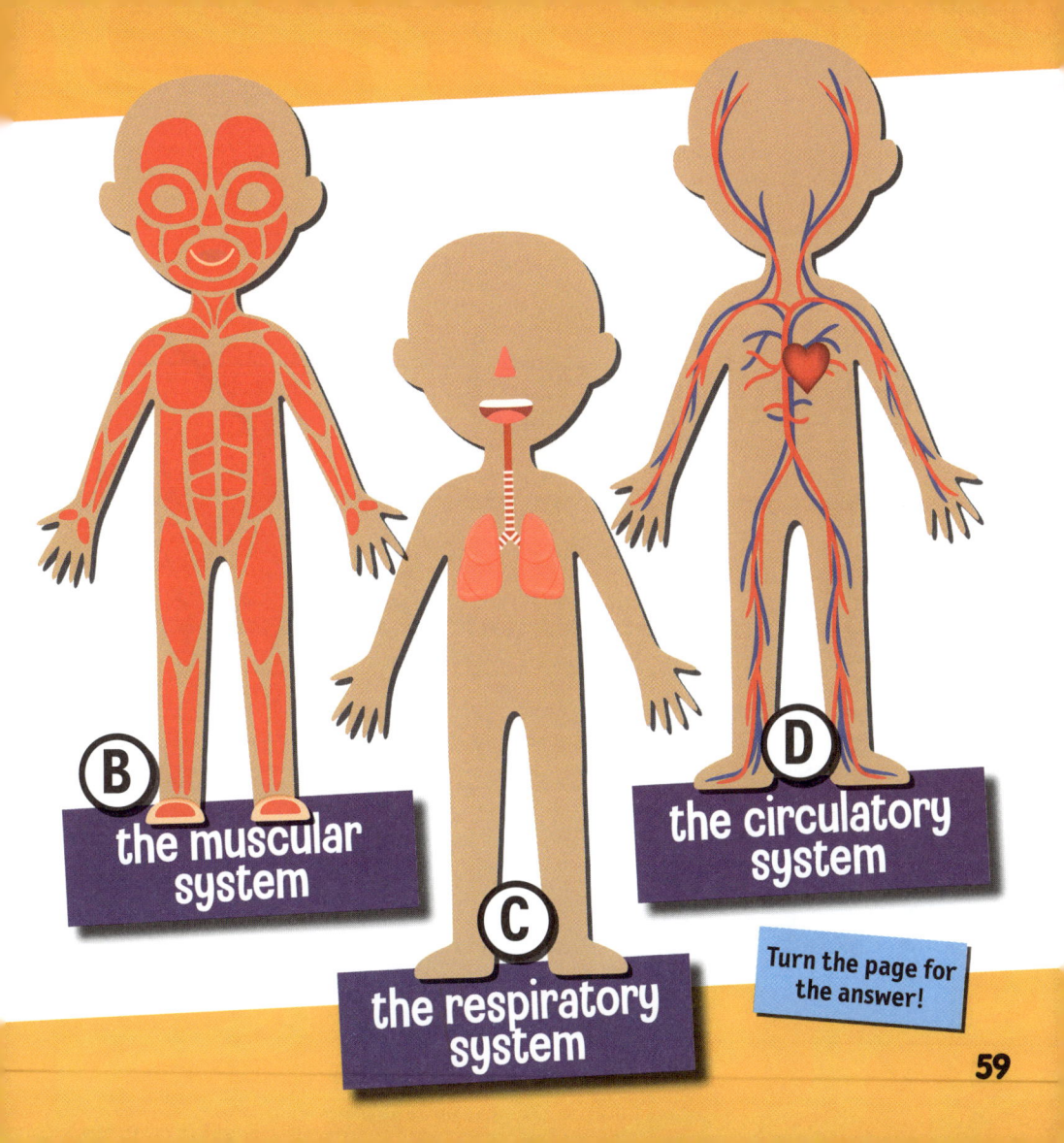

B the muscular system

C the respiratory system

D the circulatory system

Turn the page for the answer!

59

ANSWER: D the circulatory system

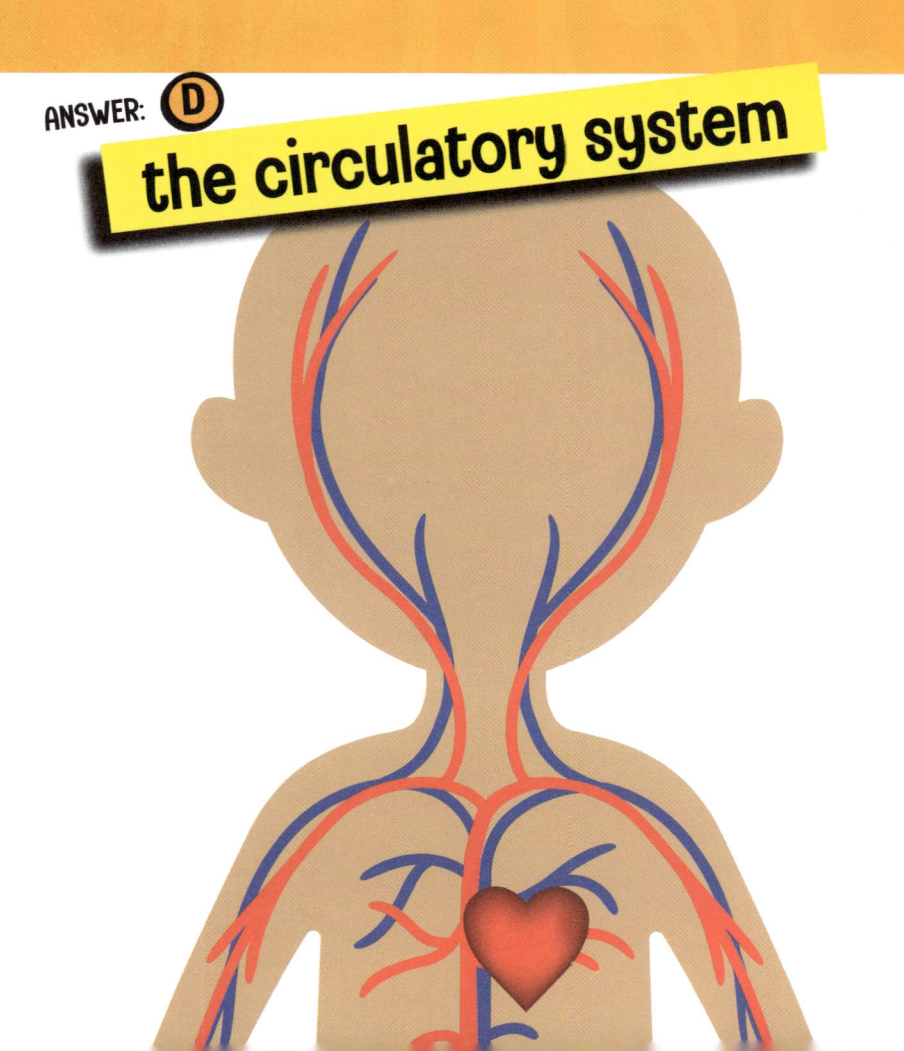

60

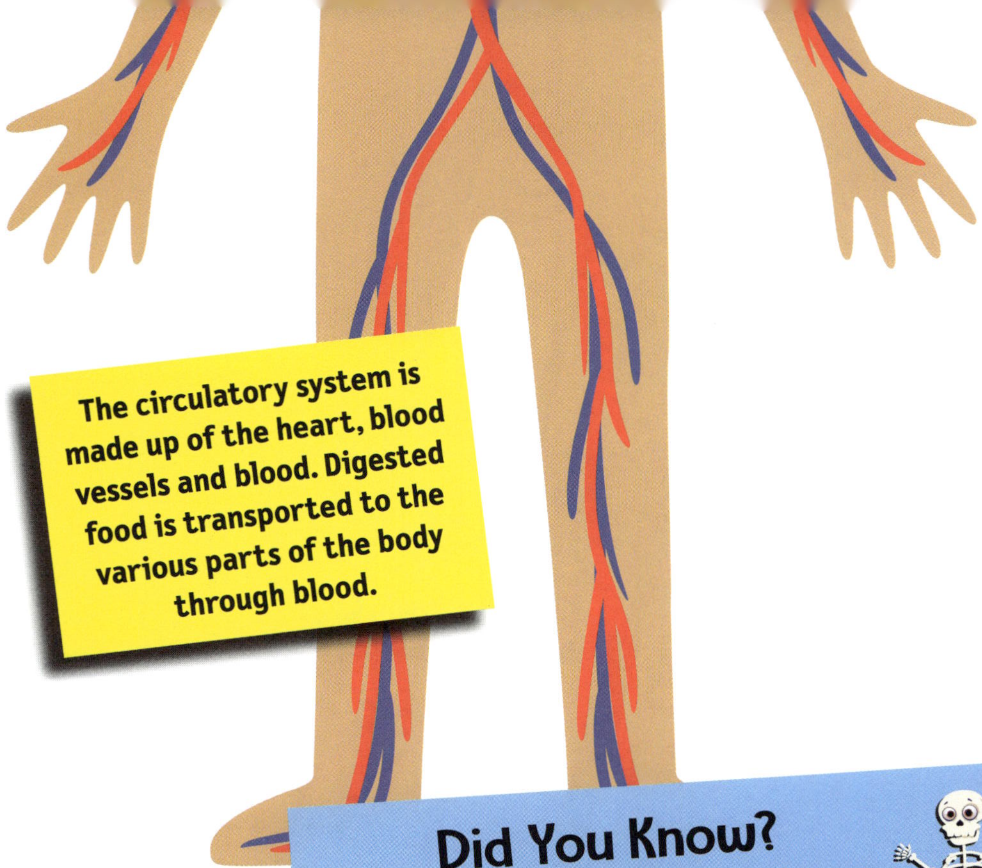

The circulatory system is made up of the heart, blood vessels and blood. Digested food is transported to the various parts of the body through blood.

Did You Know?

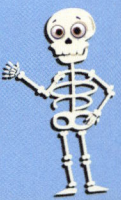

If all the blood vessels in your body were laid out end to end, they would circle the Earth two and a half times.

61

How do fruits and vegetables keep your body healthy?

What kind of furniture can we eat?

Vege-tables!

ANSWER:

They contain nutrients and fibre.

Fruits and vegetables contain important nutrients such as vitamins and minerals, which help keep us healthy. In addition, they also contain fibre. Our bodies can't digest fibre, but fibre is very important in helping to move food along the digestive system. This can help prevent constipation and maintain a healthy digestive system.

TRUE or FALSE?

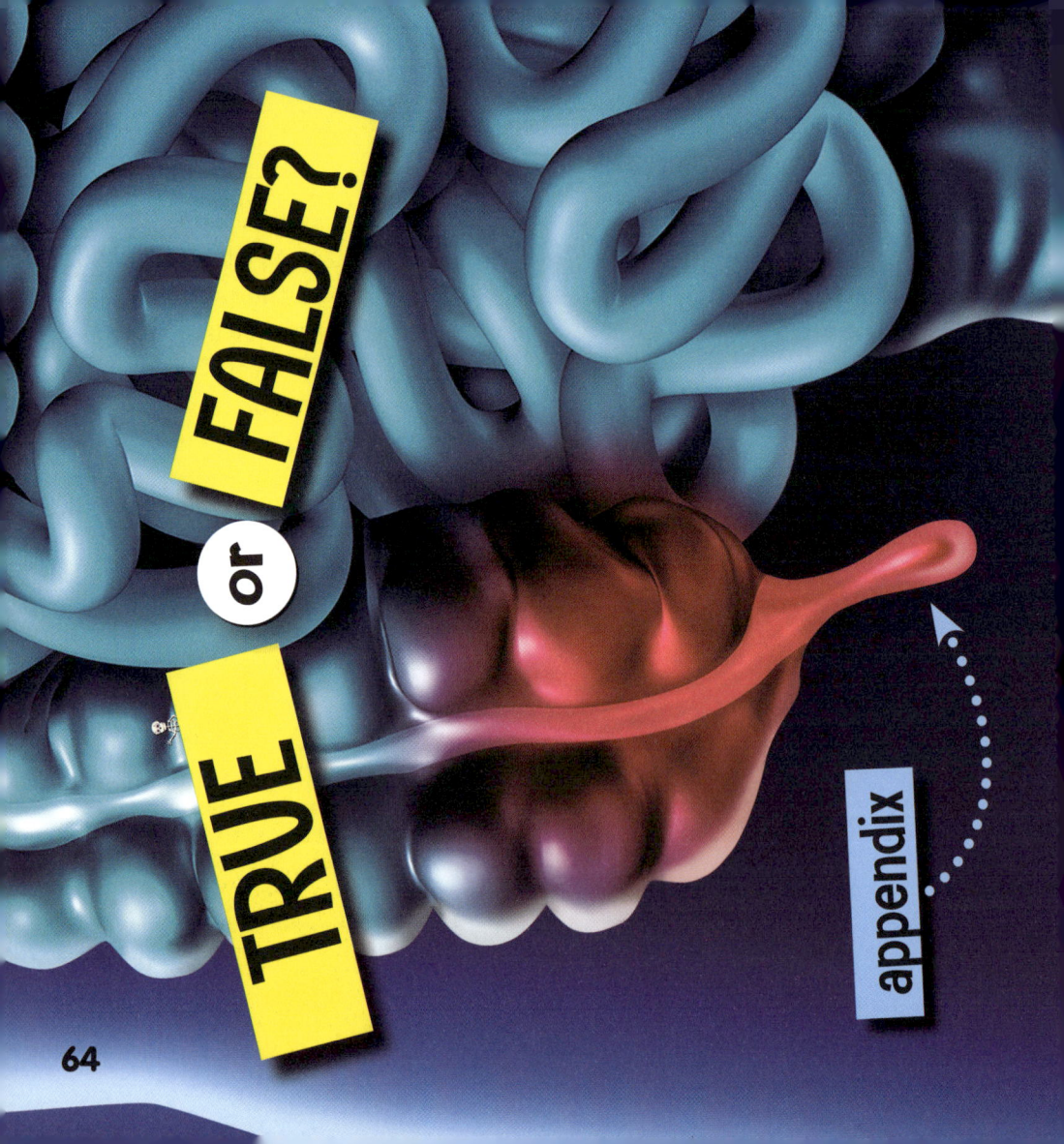

appendix

We can survive without our appendix.

ANSWER: True!

The appendix is a small, thin pouch connected to the large intestine. Its exact function is not fully understood. In some people, the appendix may get inflamed, causing pain. It can be removed by surgery without any harm caused to the body.

Why do we fart?

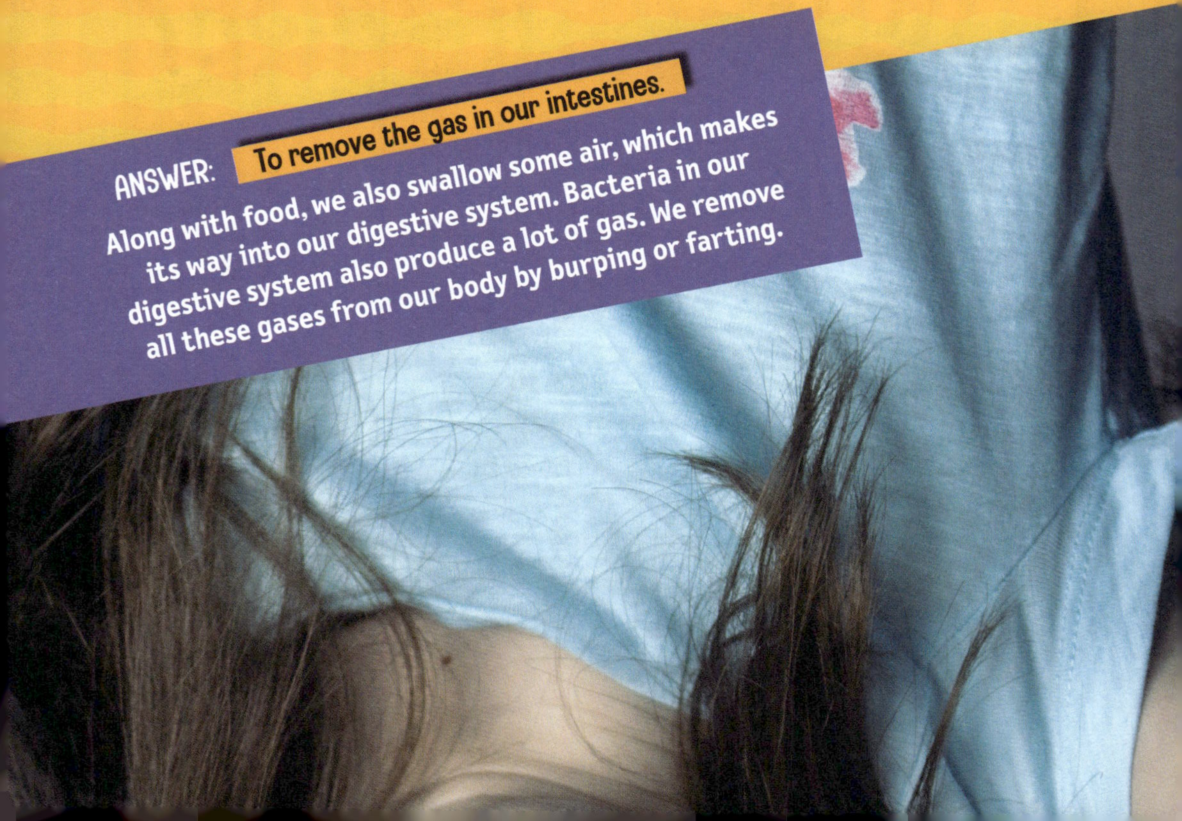

ANSWER: To remove the gas in our intestines.

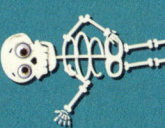

Along with food, we also swallow some air, which makes its way into our digestive system. Bacteria in our digestive system also produce a lot of gas. We remove all these gases from our body by burping or farting.

Did You Know?

Certain foods, such as beans, lentils and peas, make you fart more!

TRUE or FALSE?

Your poop contains living bacteria.

ANSWER: True!

Poop, or faeces, is mostly made of water. The rest is made of dead and living bacteria, undigested matter such as cellulose (a type of fibre), and other substances.

What did the poop say to the fart?

You blow me away!

Which body system allows us to breathe?

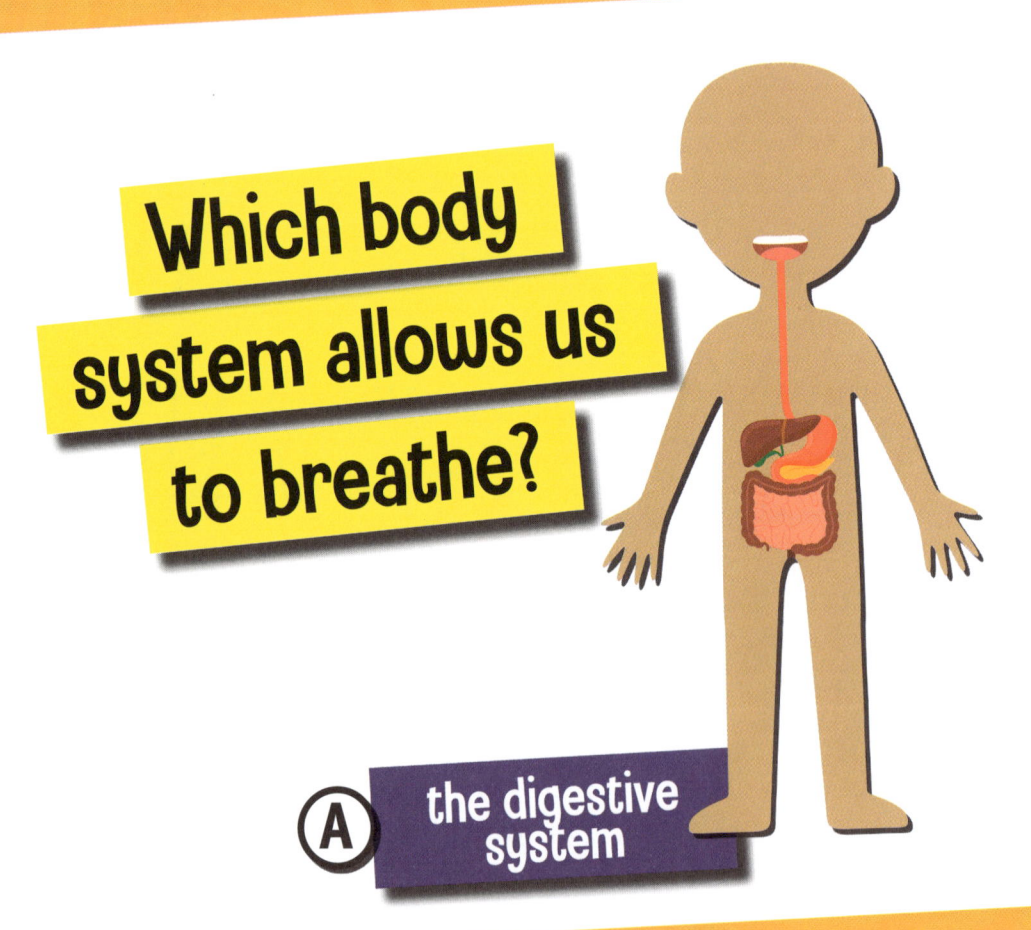

Ⓐ the digestive system

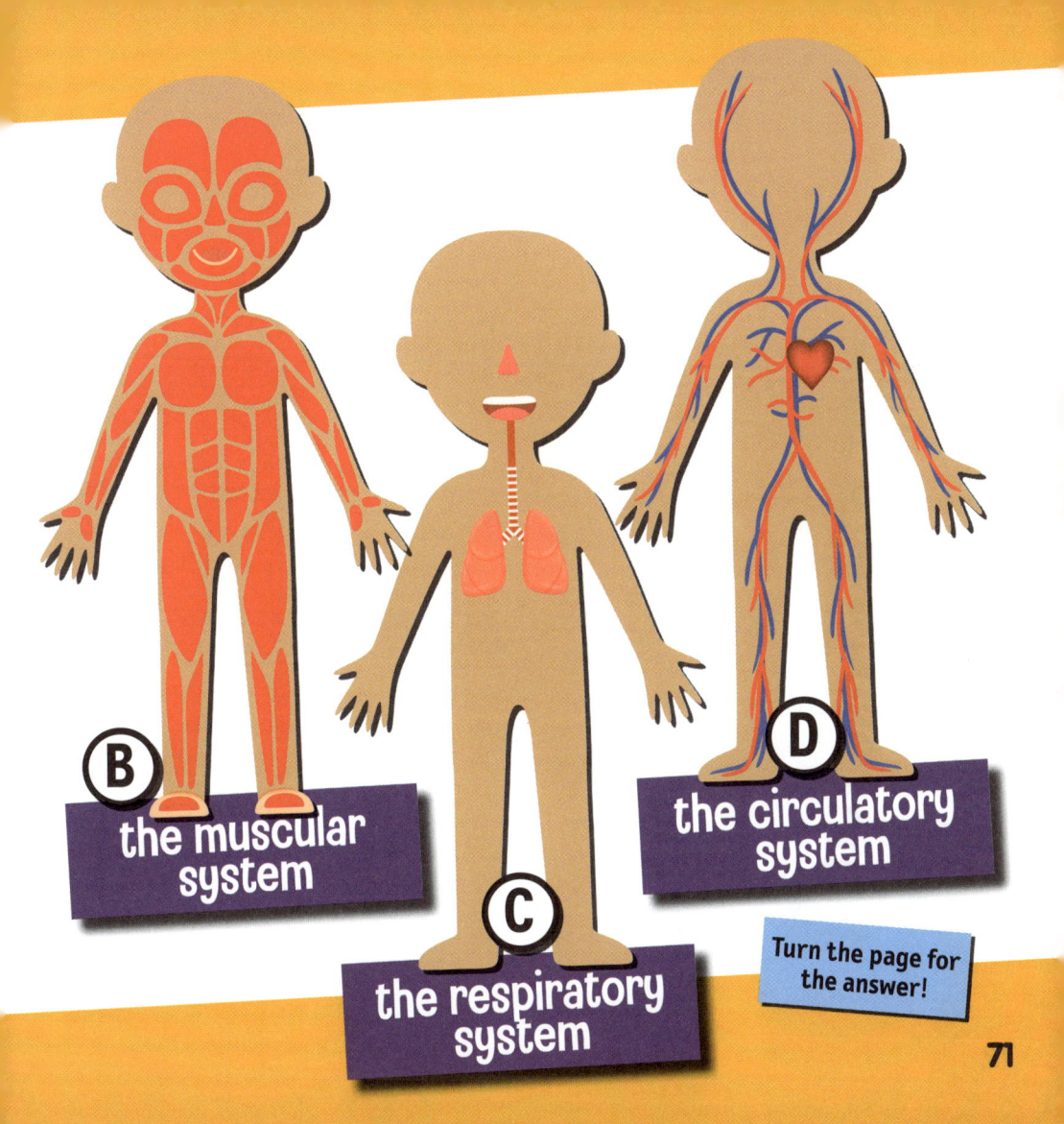

B the muscular system

C the respiratory system

D the circulatory system

Turn the page for the answer!

71

ANSWER: **C** the respiratory system

72

Our respiratory system is made up of organs such as the nose, windpipe and lungs. The respiratory system allows the body to exchange gases such as oxygen and carbon dioxide with the surroundings.

Why was the nose out of breath?

It had been running!

TRUE or FALSE?

We breathe in only oxygen from the air.

ANSWER: False!

We breathe in air, which is a mixture of gases, including oxygen. When the air reaches our lungs, oxygen is absorbed into our bloodstream. We also breathe in particles found in air, such as dust.

Did You Know?

Haze occurs when there are too many particles such as dust and smoke in the air, affecting visibility. These particles can enter our respiratory system and make us ill. We should avoid going outdoors during haze. Many people wear a mask if they have to go outdoors.

Which gas is air mostly made up of?

- **A** oxygen
- **B** nitrogen
- **C** water vapour
- **D** carbon dioxide

ANSWER: (B) nitrogen

Nitrogen makes up about 78% of the air around us. Oxygen makes up about 21%. The remaining 1% is made up of carbon dioxide, argon, water vapour and other gases.

TRUE or FALSE?

Your two lungs are exactly the same size.

Turn the page for the answer!

78

Why were the lungs so tired?

They worked lung hours!

79

Your left lung is smaller than your right lung to accommodate the heart.

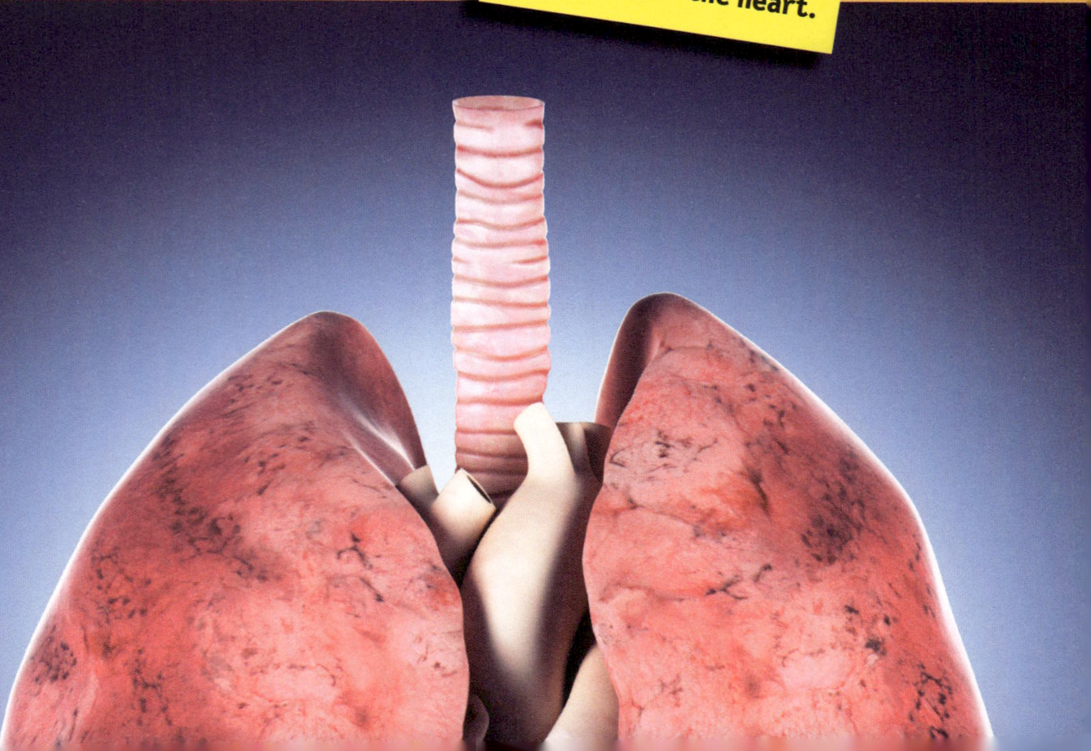

ANSWER: **False!**

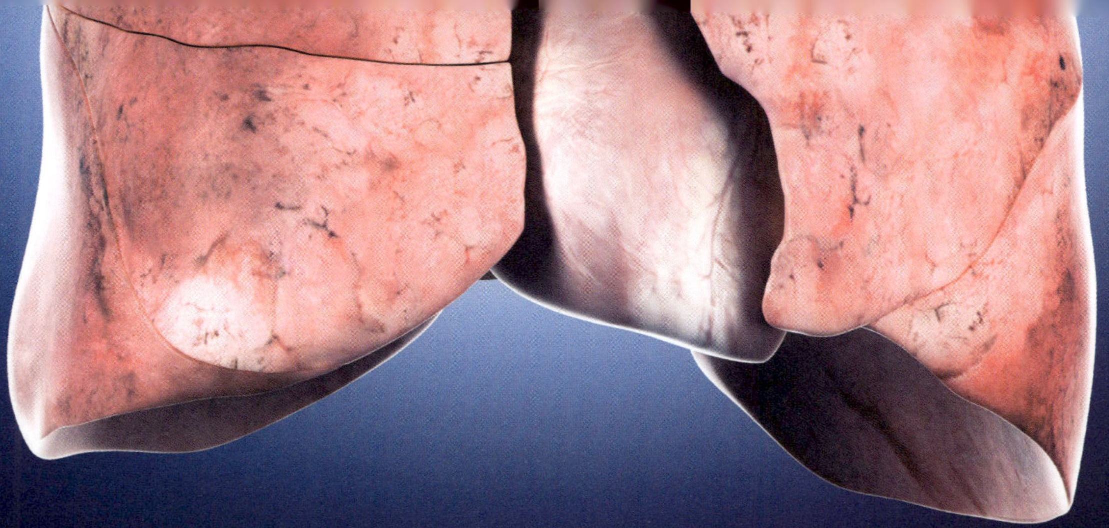

What did the left lung say to the right lung?

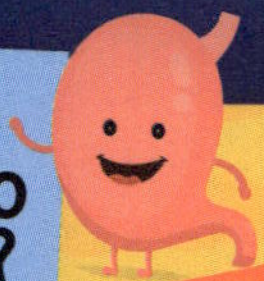

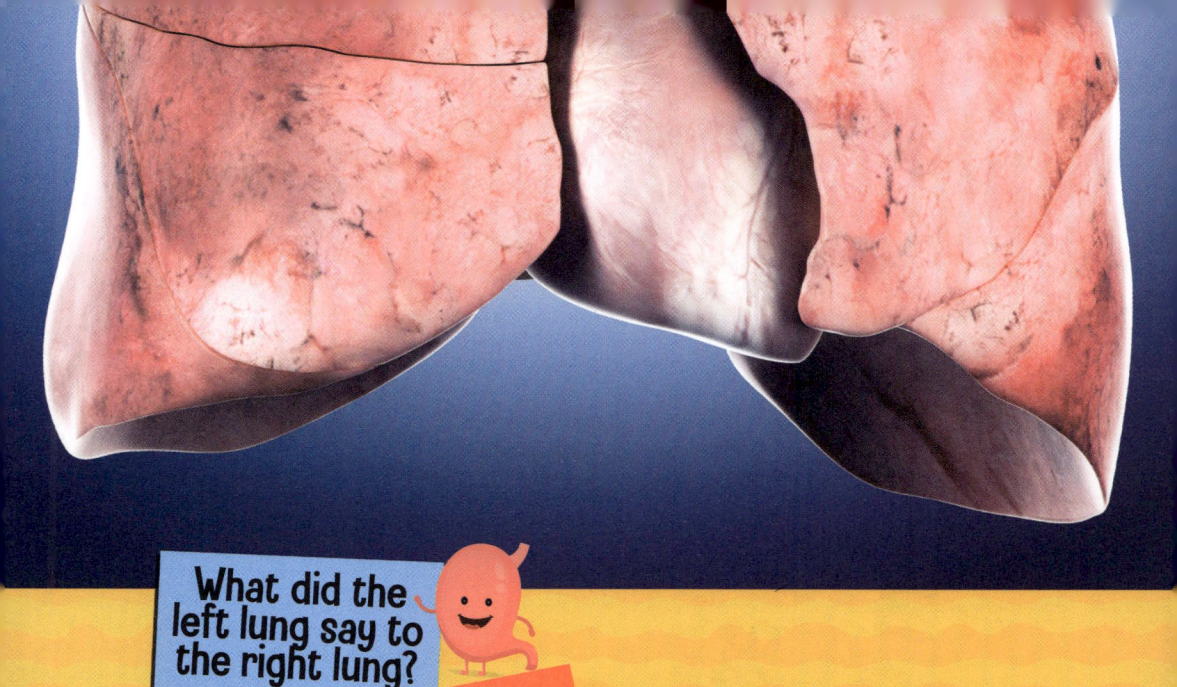

We be-lung together!

Did You Know?

Lungs have a very large surface area for exchange of gases. In fact, if a pair of lungs were opened flat, they would cover an entire tennis court!

Why do we have nose hair?

ANSWER:
To act as a filter.

The hairs in our noses act as a filter. A thin layer of a slimy substance called mucus around the hairs traps dust, germs and other particles. This prevents them from entering our lungs and causing any harm.

What do cows have in their noses?

Moo-cus!

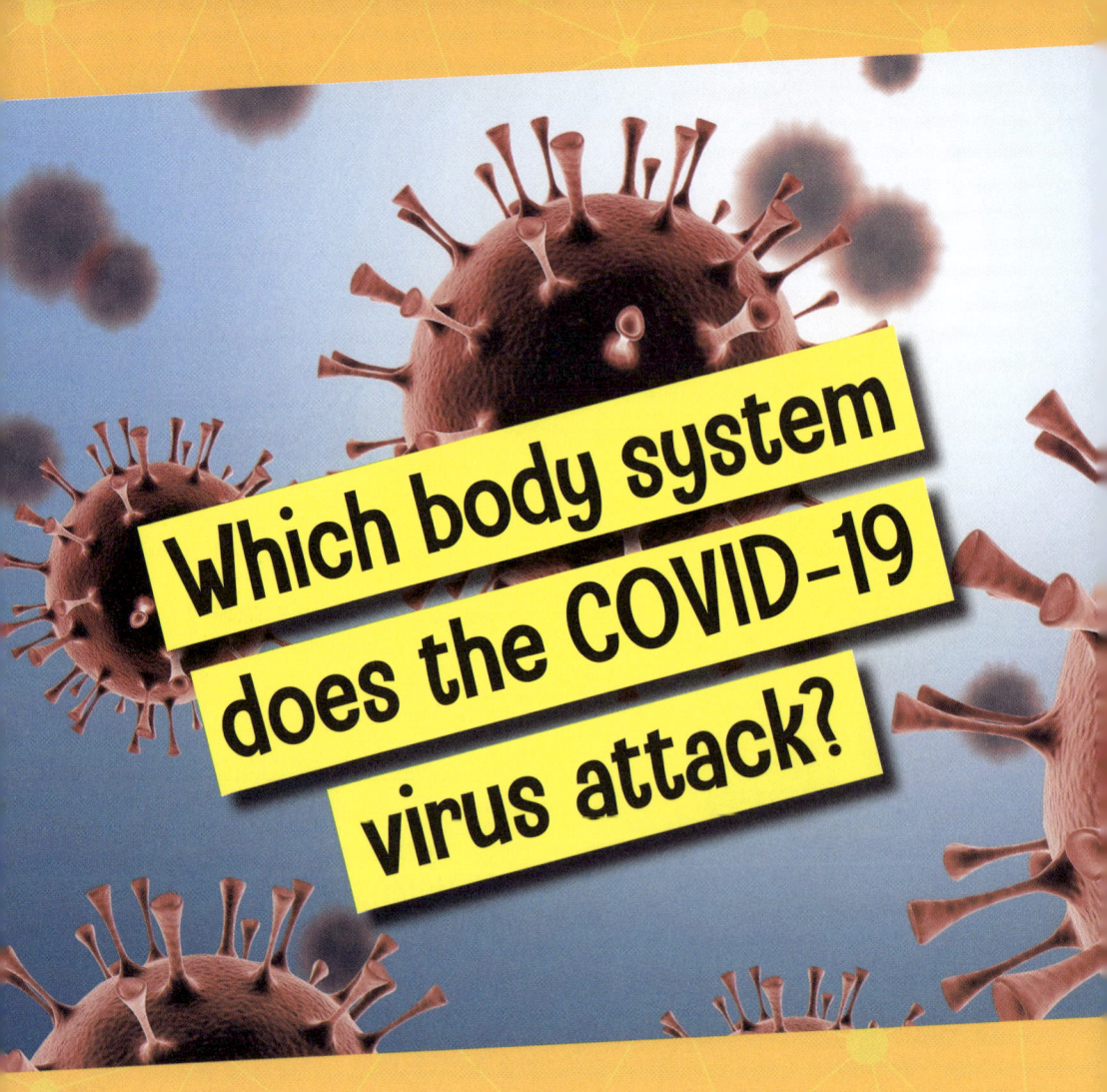

Which body system does the COVID-19 virus attack?

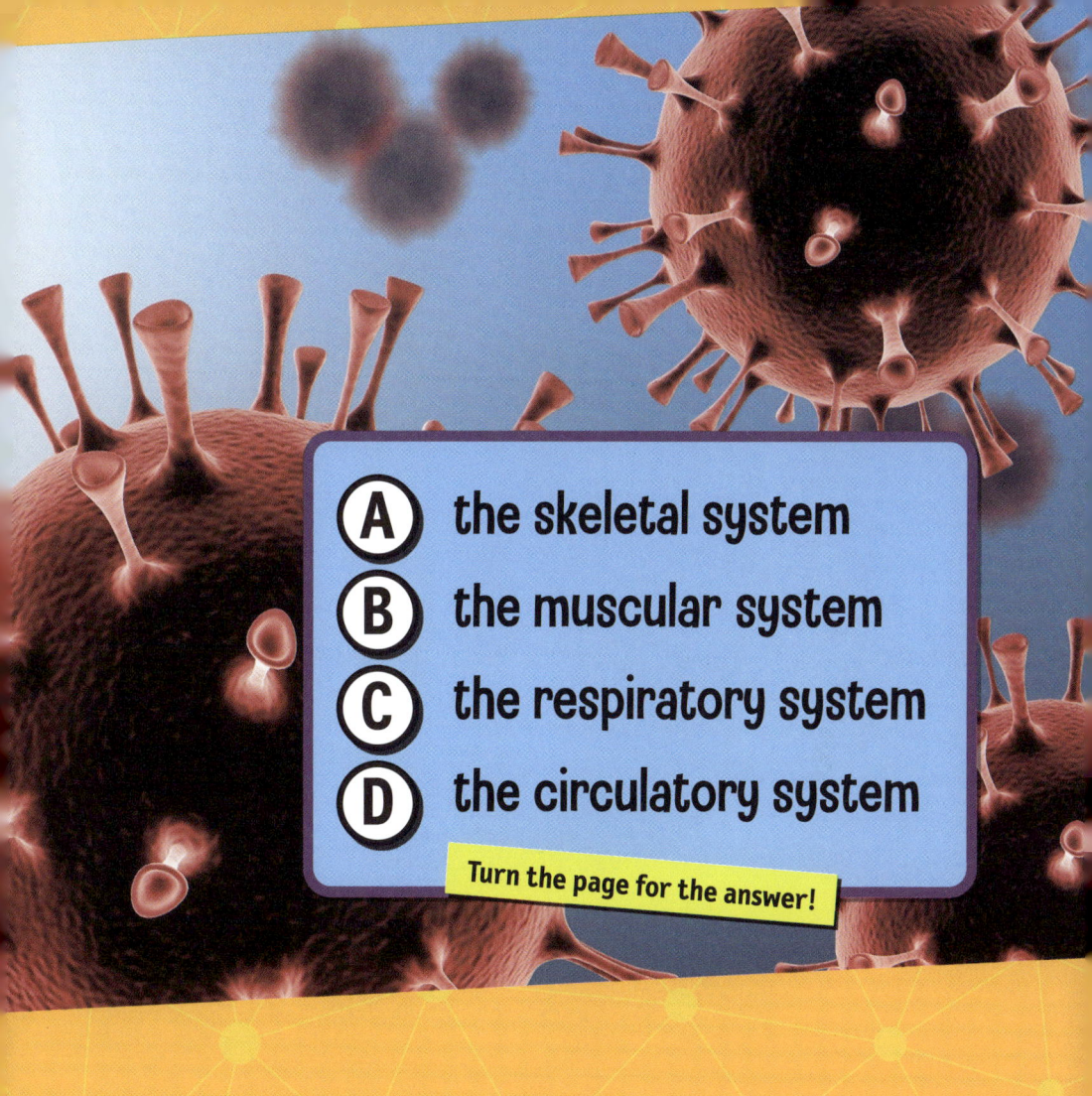

A the skeletal system

B the muscular system

C the respiratory system

D the circulatory system

Turn the page for the answer!

ANSWER: C

the respiratory system

86

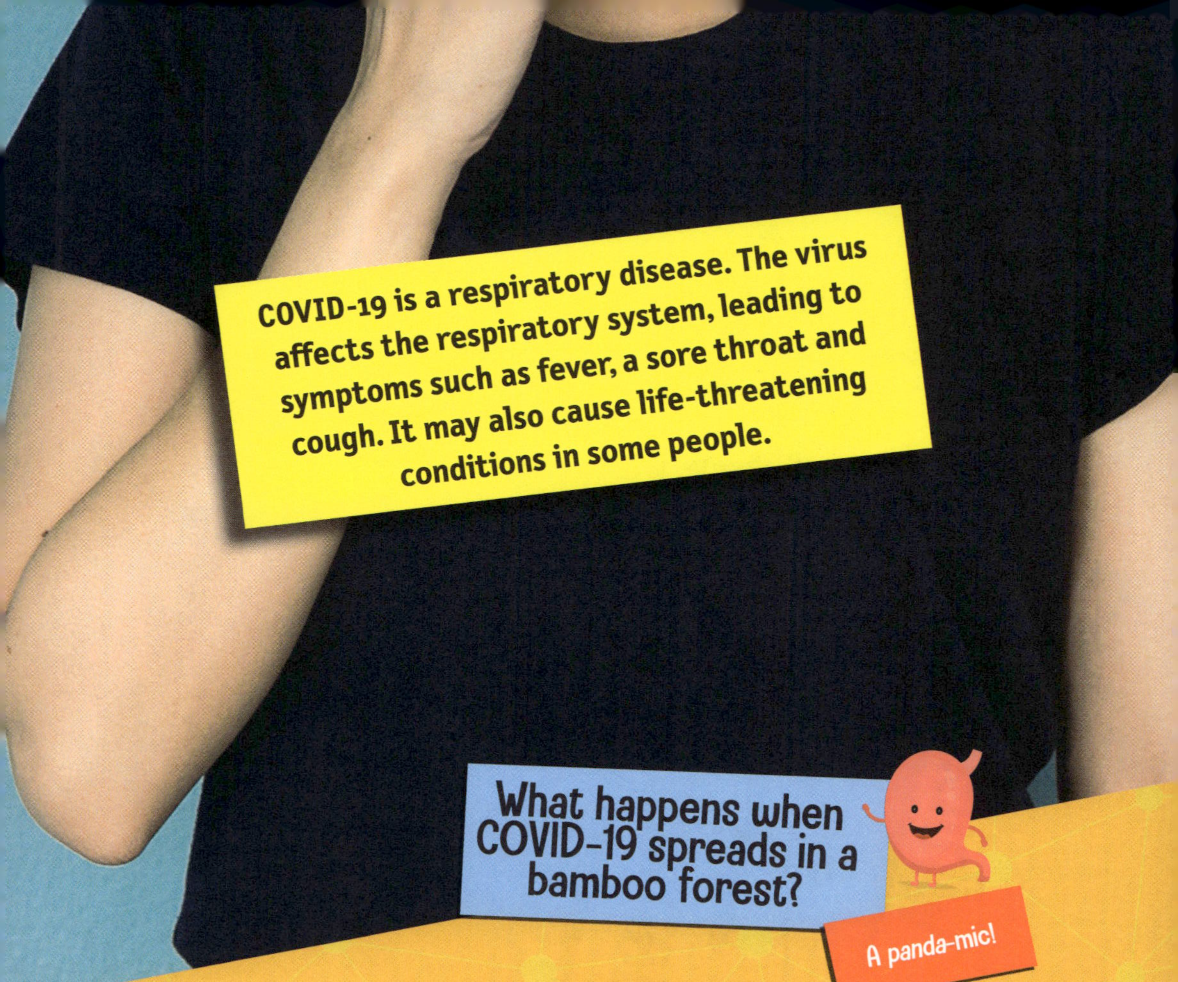

COVID-19 is a respiratory disease. The virus affects the respiratory system, leading to symptoms such as fever, a sore throat and cough. It may also cause life-threatening conditions in some people.

What happens when COVID-19 spreads in a bamboo forest?

A panda-mic!

Which picture shows lungs damaged by smoking?

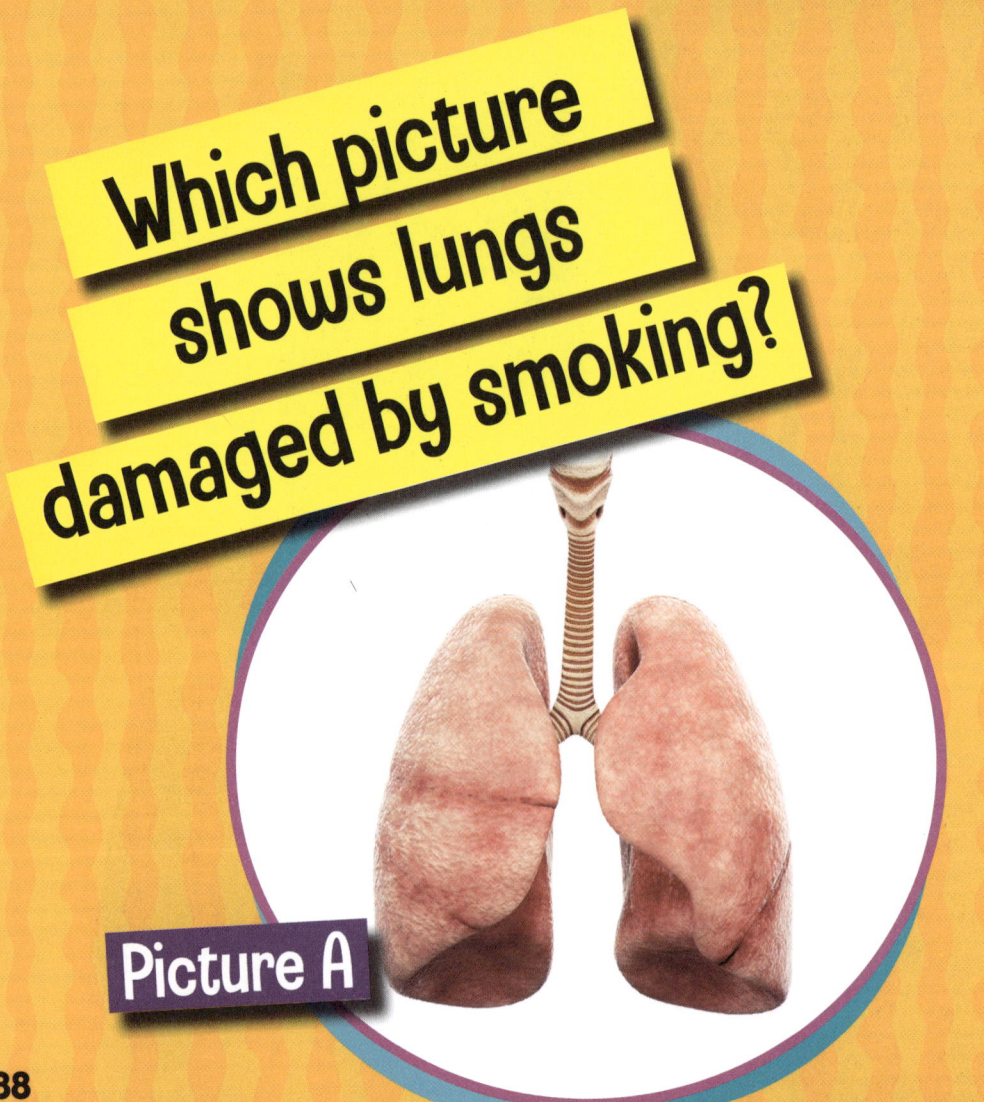

Picture A

88

Picture B

Did You Know?

Smoking is not only harmful for smokers, but for those around them as well. Breathing in a smoker's tobacco smoke is known as passive smoking.

ANSWER: Picture B. Cigarettes contain a large amount of chemicals. Smoking can cause these chemicals to enter the lungs and damage them. Years of smoking may also cause sticky tar to be deposited in the lungs, giving them a dark colour.

TRUE or FALSE?

A human can survive with only one lung.

90

ANSWER: True!

Both our lungs have the same function. Diseases such as lung cancer can lead to a lung being removed. Most people can live an almost normal life with one lung. However, the ability to exercise like before is likely to be affected.

Did You Know?

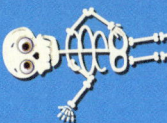

An average human takes about 22,000 breaths in a day.

Which body system is this?

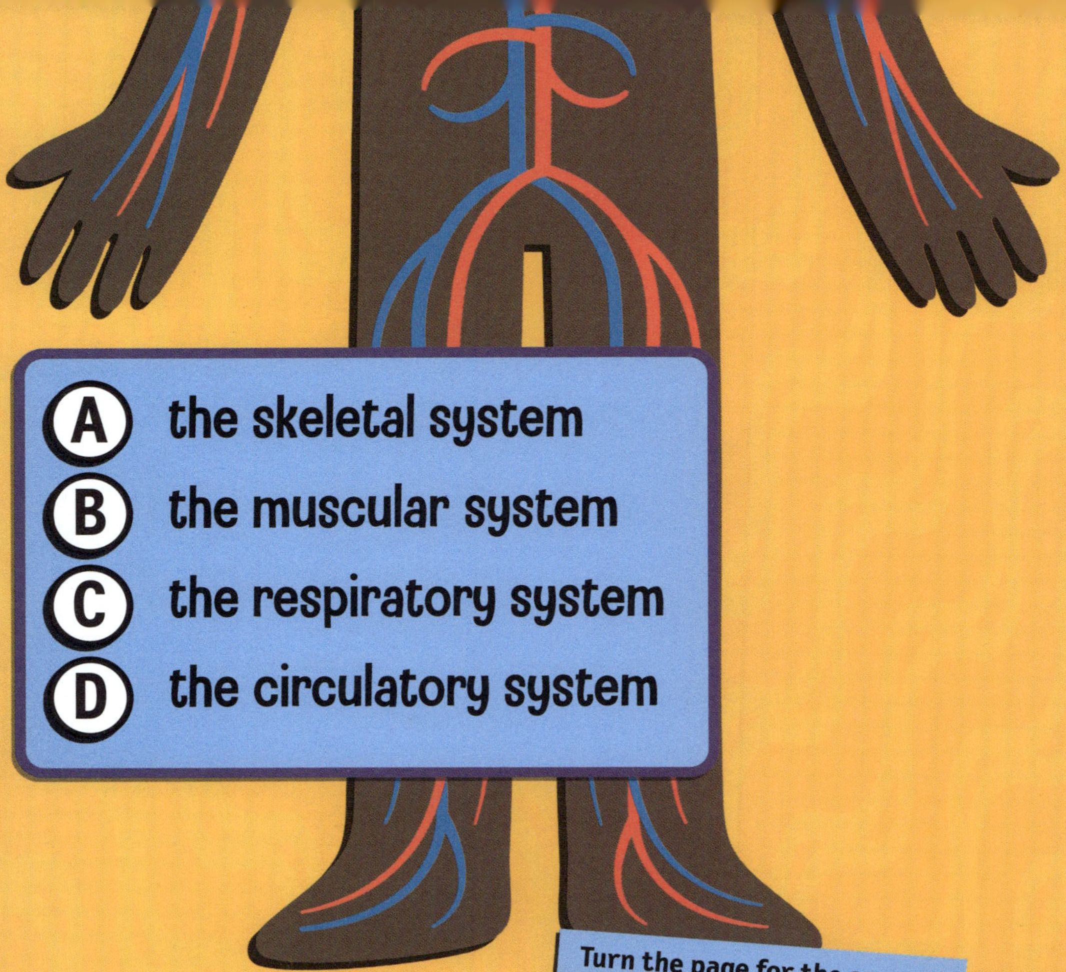

- **A** the skeletal system
- **B** the muscular system
- **C** the respiratory system
- **D** the circulatory system

Turn the page for the answer!

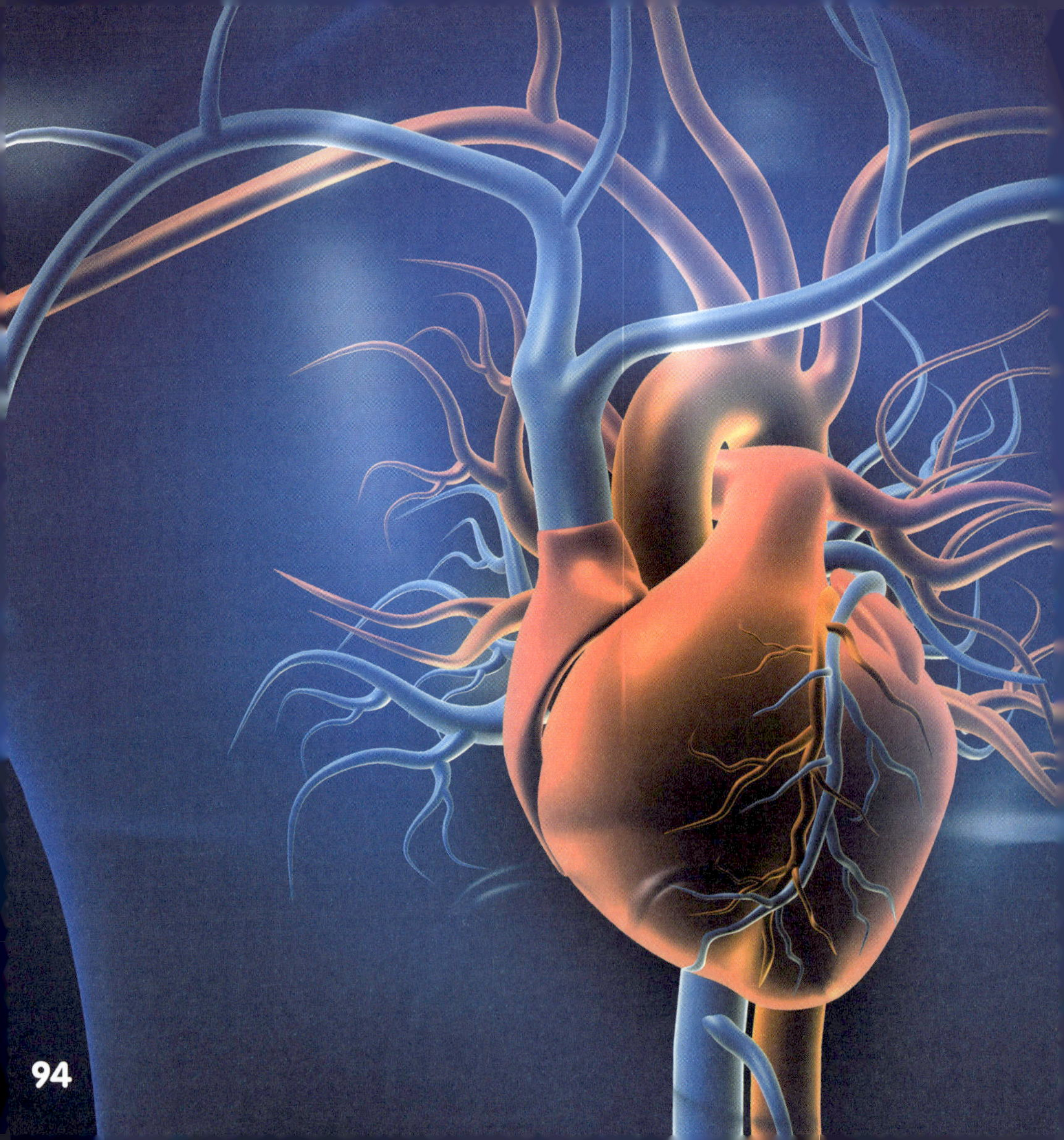

ANSWER: **D**

the circulatory system

The circulatory system is made up of organs such as the heart and blood vessels. Blood in the blood vessels transports substances such as oxygen, digested food and waste materials around the body.

Did You Know?
Your heart is the size of your fist!

How much blood is in the adult human body?

A about 1 litre

B about 3 litres

C about 5 litres

D about 10 litres

ANSWER: **C** about 5 litres

The average adult human has about 5 litres of blood in the body. Blood is made up of a fluid called plasma, and cells such as red blood cells, white blood cells and platelets.

97

Which of these are NOT blood vessels?

A) veins
B) arteries
C) platelets
D) capillaries

98

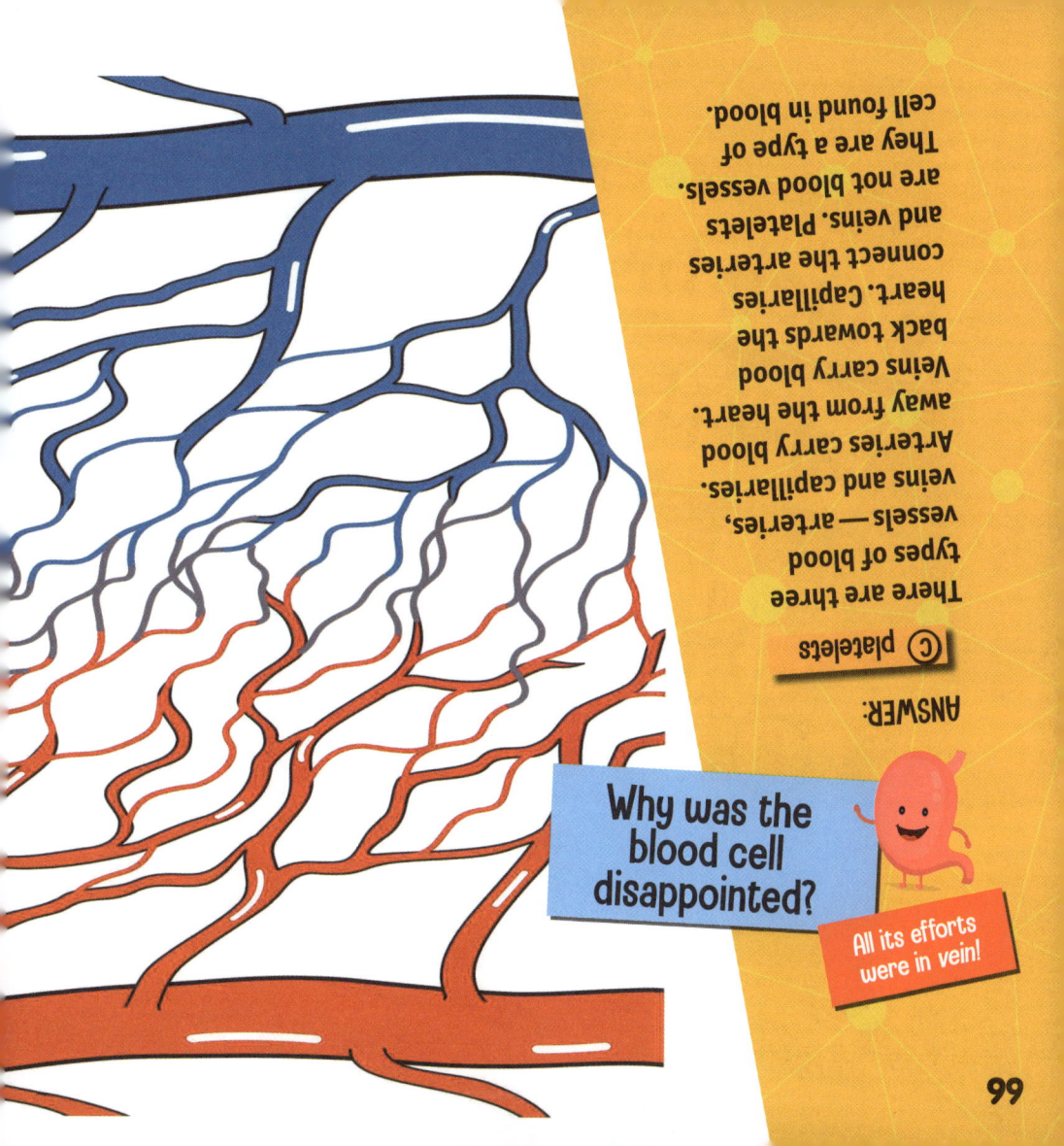

There are three types of blood vessels — arteries, veins and capillaries. Arteries carry blood away from the heart. Veins carry blood back towards the heart. Capillaries connect the arteries and veins. Platelets are not blood vessels. They are a type of cell found in blood.

ANSWER:

C) platelets

Why was the blood cell disappointed?

All its efforts were in vein!

Which blood vessels are the smallest?

- **A** veins
- **B** arteries
- **C** capillaries

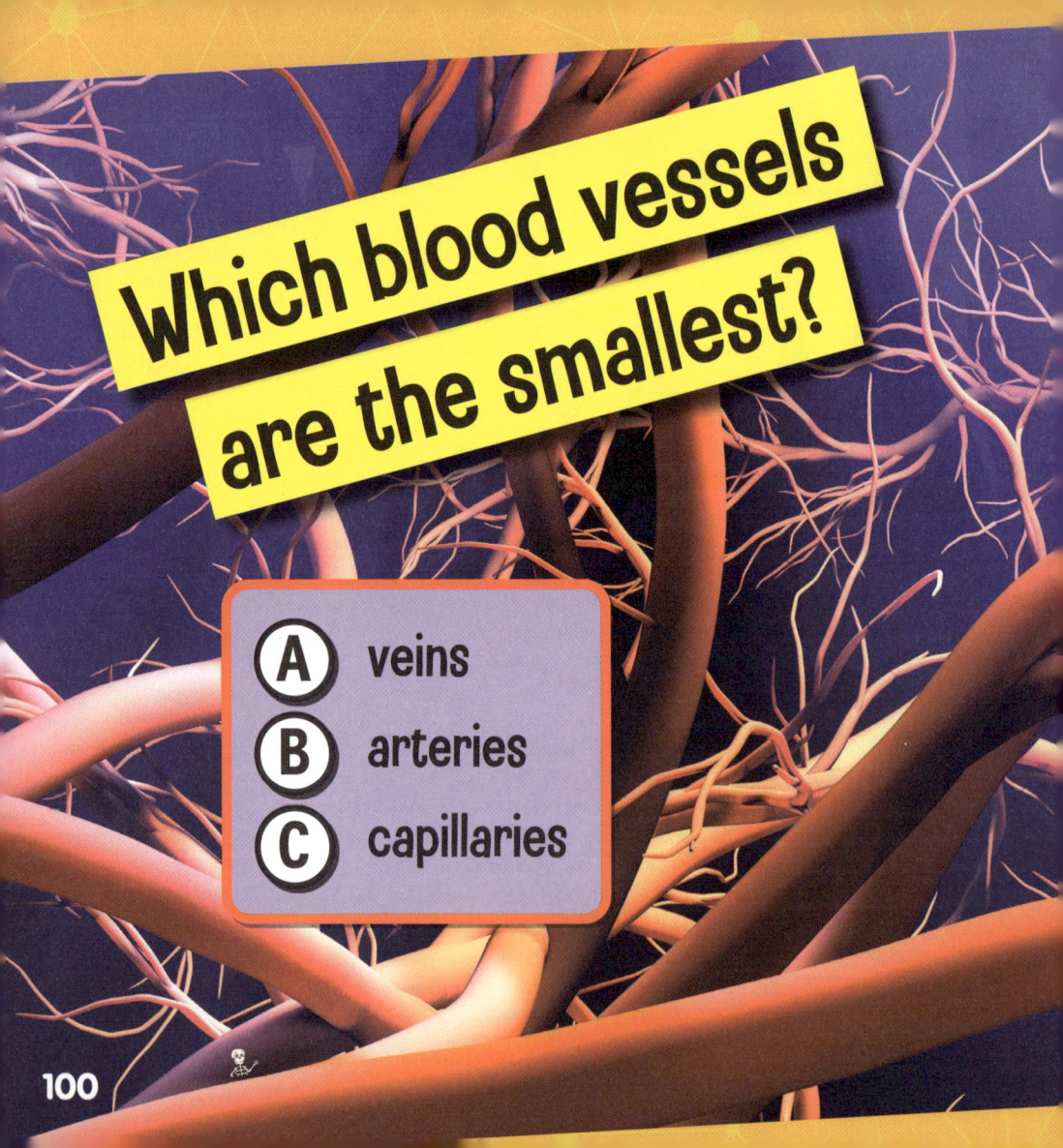

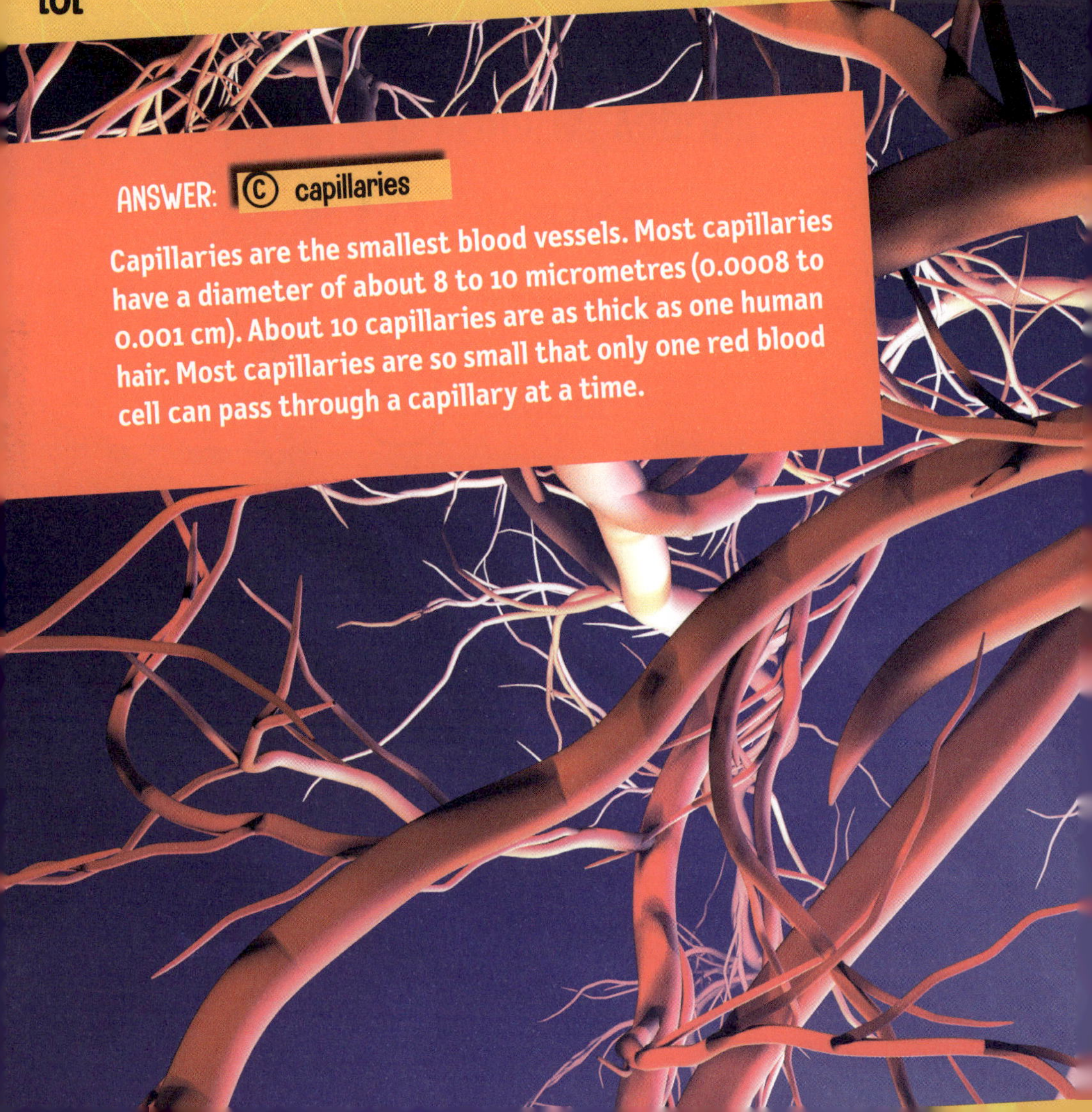

ANSWER: C) capillaries

Capillaries are the smallest blood vessels. Most capillaries have a diameter of about 8 to 10 micrometres (0.0008 to 0.001 cm). About 10 capillaries are as thick as one human hair. Most capillaries are so small that only one red blood cell can pass through a capillary at a time.

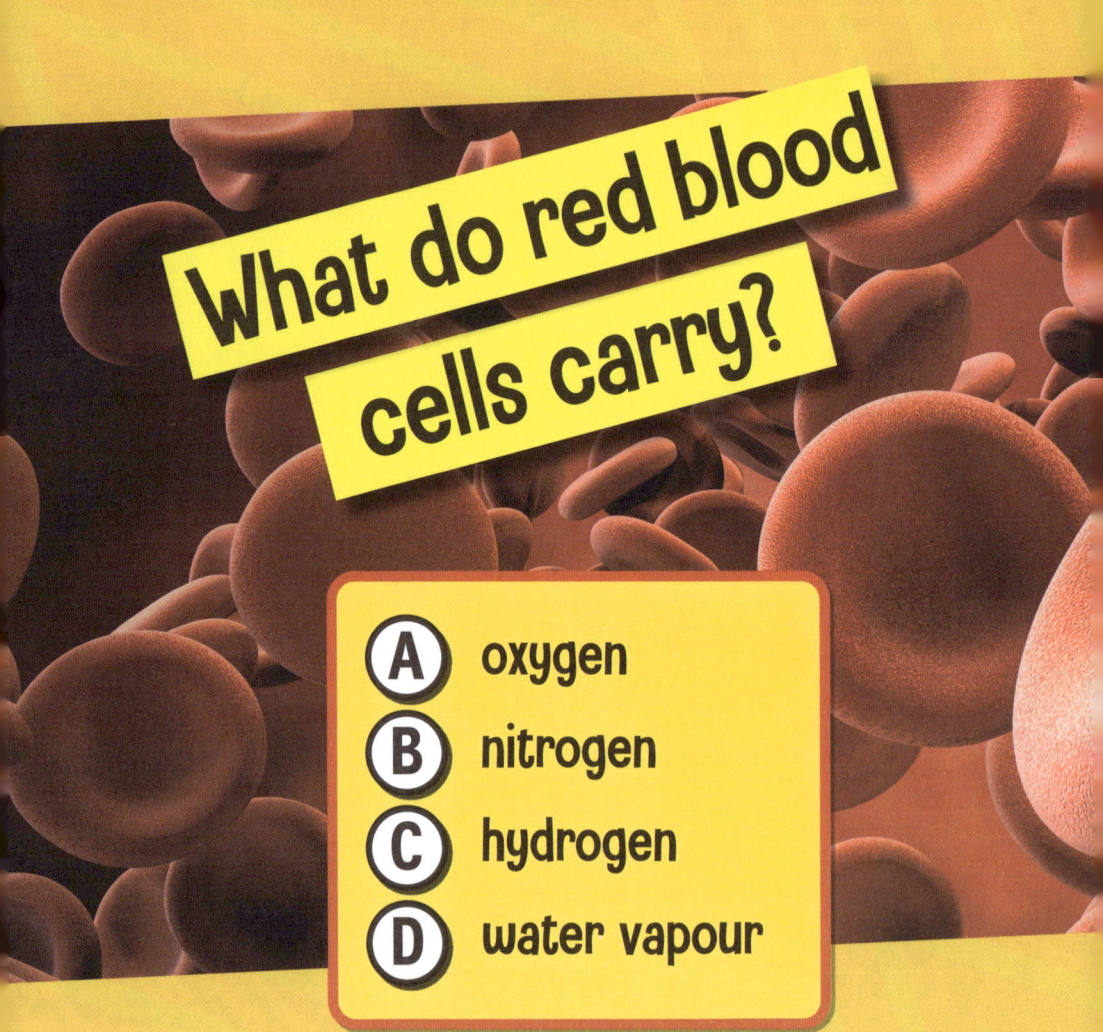

What do red blood cells carry?

- **A** oxygen
- **B** nitrogen
- **C** hydrogen
- **D** water vapour

ANSWER: Ⓐ **oxygen**

Your blood is made of four main components — a fluid called plasma, red blood cells, white blood cells and platelets. Red blood cells are responsible for carrying oxygen to various parts of your body. All cells of your body need oxygen to carry out their functions. Red blood cells also carry carbon dioxide to the lungs to be exhaled.

Did You Know?

Blood cells are produced in bone marrow. Bone marrow is the soft, spongy material found in the centre of your bones.

What do you call it when a red blood cell runs away?

A marrow escape!

103

Which component of blood fights germs?

- **A** plasma
- **B** platelets
- **C** red blood cells
- **D** white blood cells

platelet

red blood cell

Turn the page for the answer!

104

composition of blood

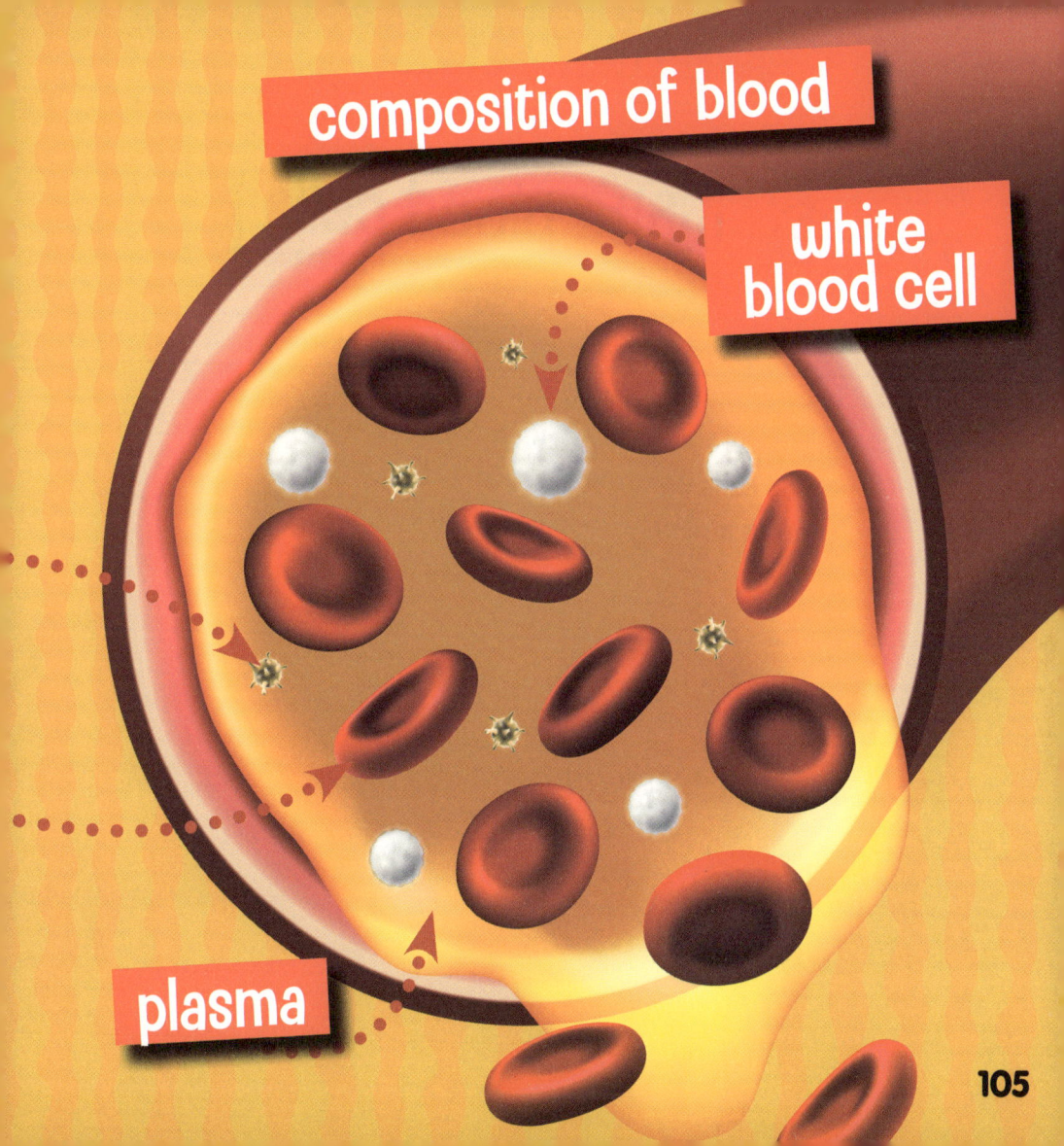

white blood cell

plasma

ANSWER: **D** **white blood cells**

White blood cells are an important part of your immune system. This is the system that protects your body from infections. White blood cells fight germs such as bacteria and viruses and help keep you healthy.

Did You Know?

When you get an infection, the number of white blood cells in your blood increases to help fight the infection.

Why do white blood cells hate jokes?

Because laughter is infectious!

What is the function of platelets in the blood?

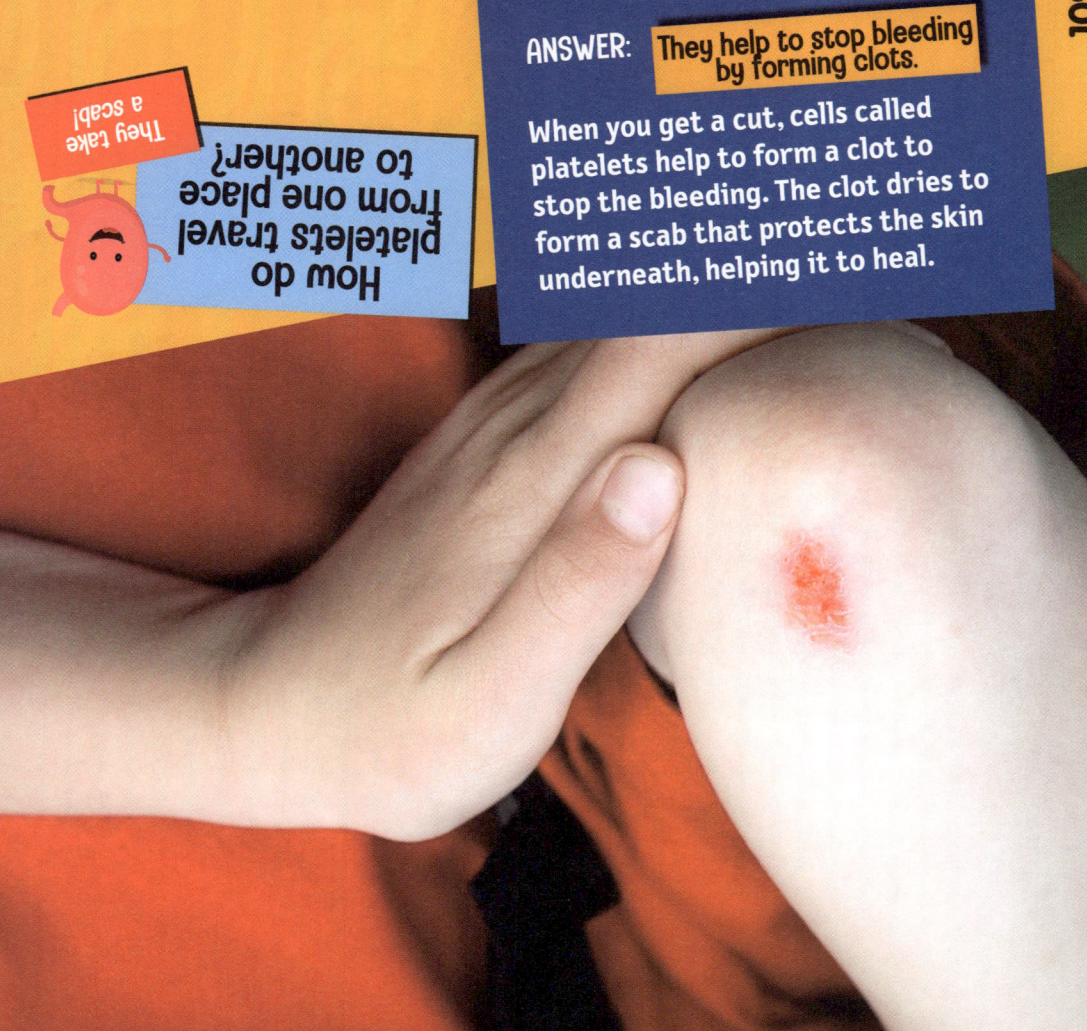

How do platelets travel from one place to another?

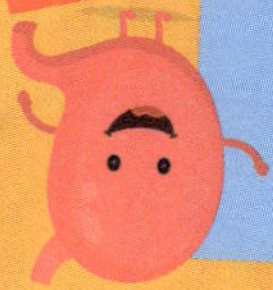

They take a scab!

ANSWER: They help to stop bleeding by forming clots.

When you get a cut, cells called platelets help to form a clot to stop the bleeding. The clot dries to form a scab that protects the skin underneath, helping it to heal.

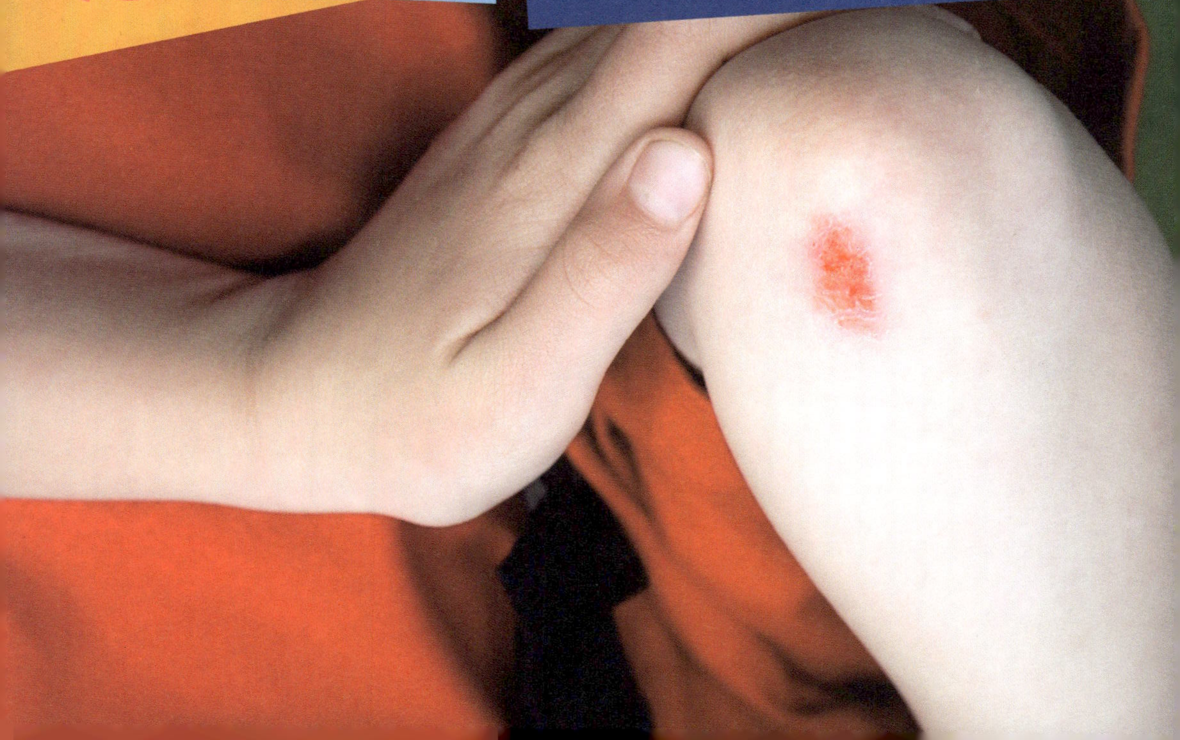

TRUE or FALSE?

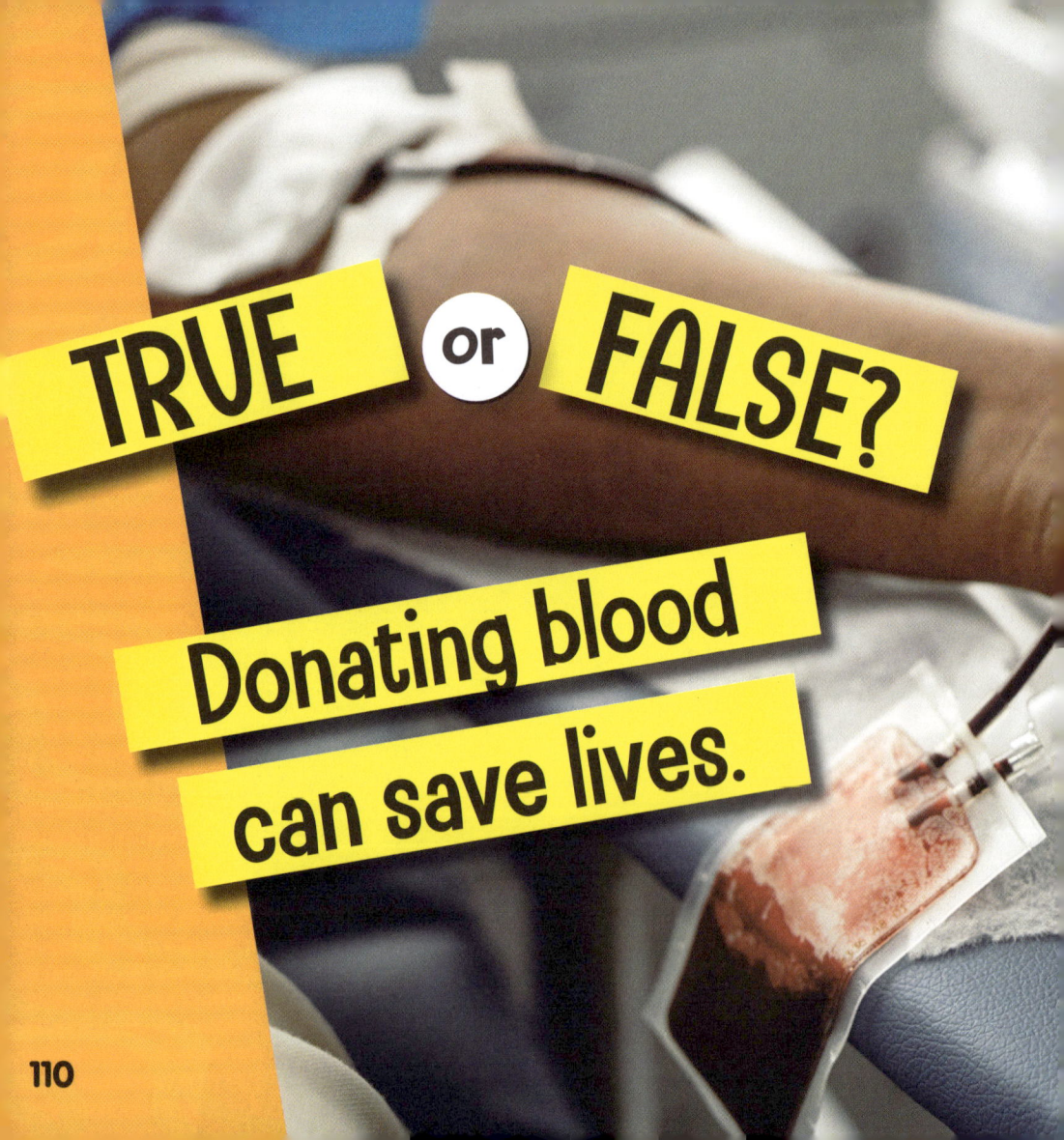

Donating blood can save lives.

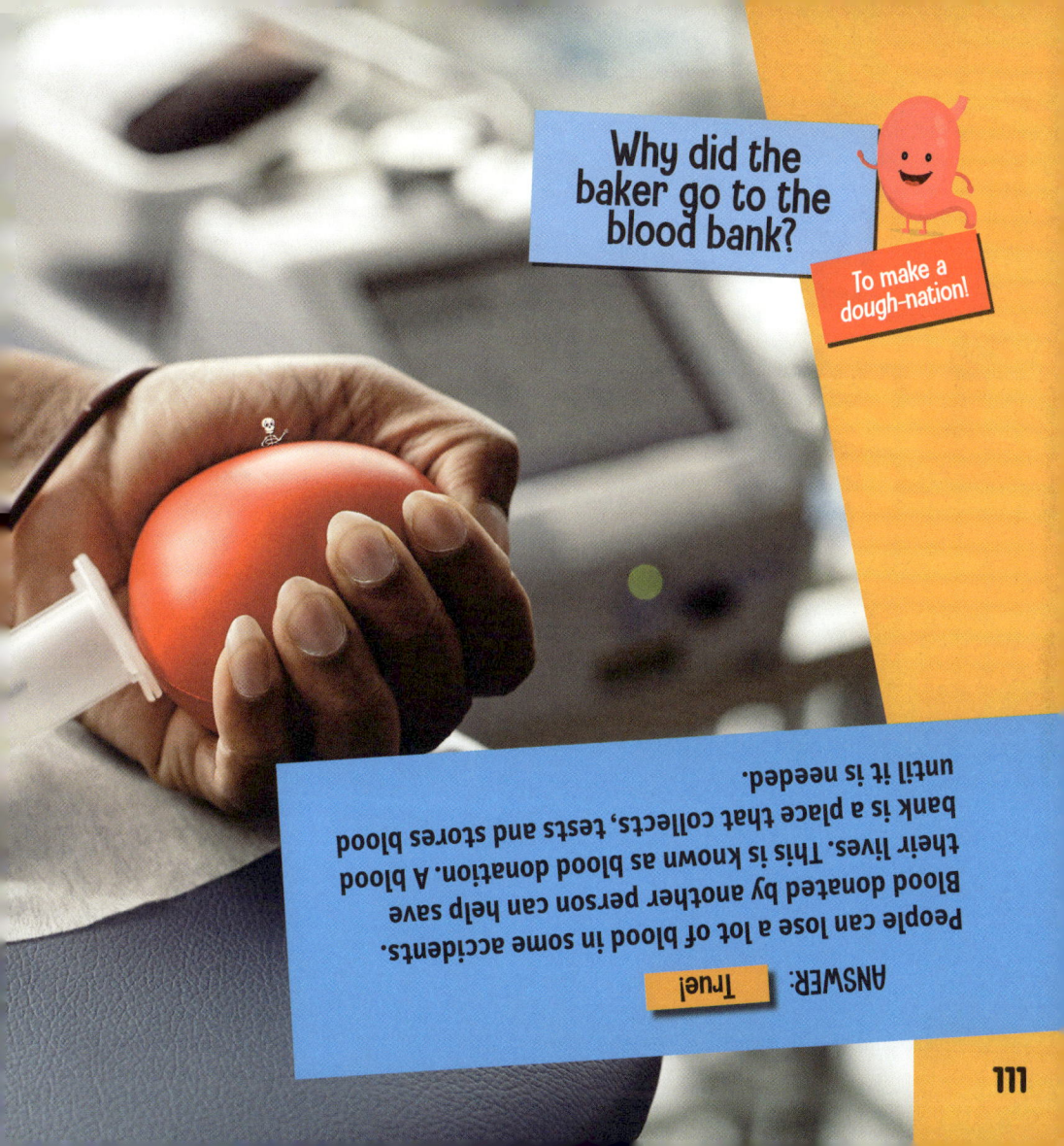

Why did the baker go to the blood bank?

To make a dough-nation!

ANSWER: True!

People can lose a lot of blood in some accidents. Blood donated by another person can help save their lives. This is known as blood donation. A blood bank is a place that collects, tests and stores blood until it is needed.

111

What is the normal resting heart rate in human adults?

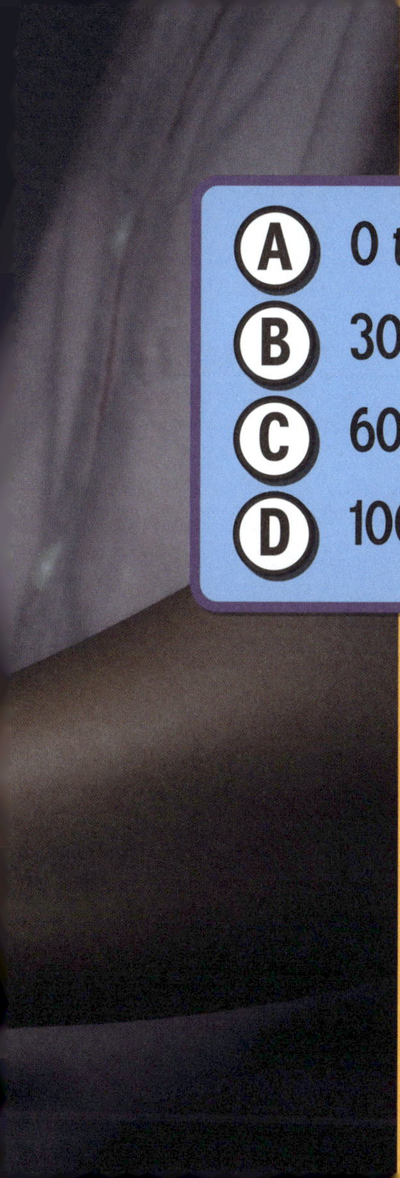

A 0 to 30 beats per minute

B 30 to 60 beats per minute

C 60 to 100 beats per minute

D 100 to 150 beats per minute

ANSWER: C 60 to 100 beats per minute

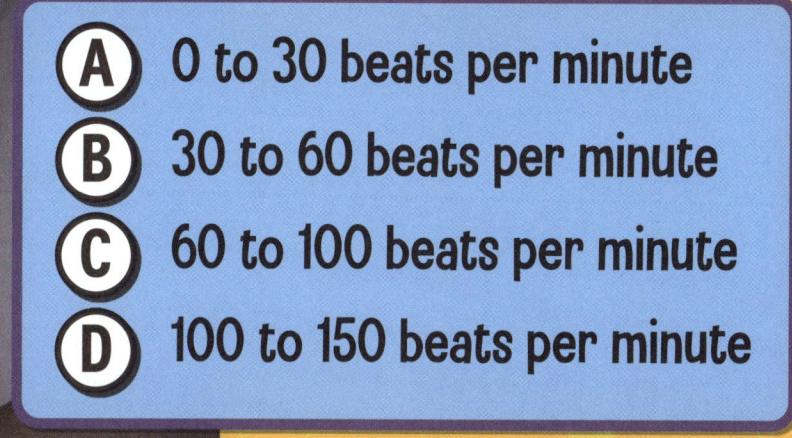

Your heart rate is the number of times your heart beats in a minute. Human adults usually have a resting heart rate of 60 to 100 beats per minute. Your heart rate increases when you exercise.

Why does your heart beat faster when you run?

Which body part can run while staying in the same place?

Your nose!

ANSWER: To supply energy to your muscles.

Your blood supplies all parts of your body with digested food and oxygen for energy. When you run, your muscles need more energy. The heart beats faster to provide the muscles with more digested food and oxygen for energy.

115

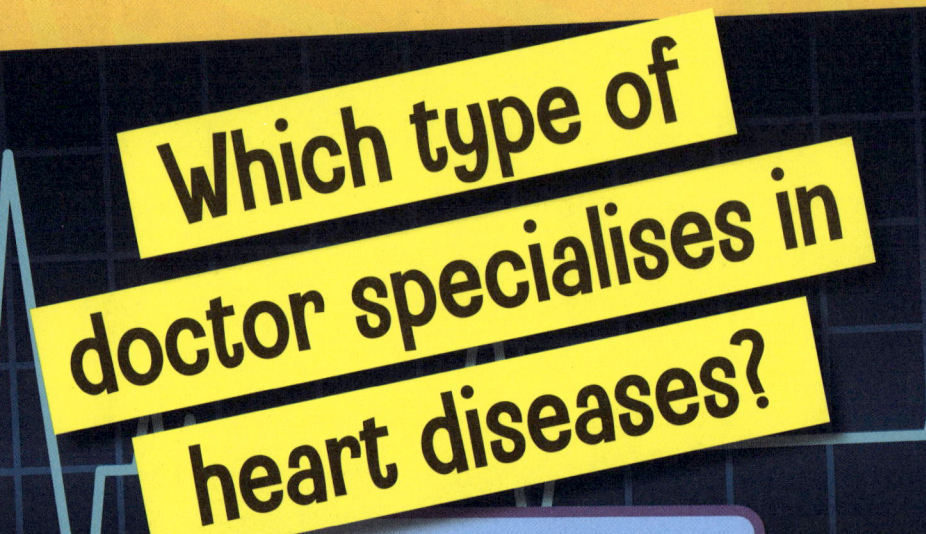

Which type of doctor specialises in heart diseases?

- **A** a dentist
- **B** a podiatrist
- **C** a neurologist
- **D** a cardiologist

ANSWER: D) a cardiologist

The word 'cardio' comes from the ancient Greek word 'kardia', which means 'heart'.

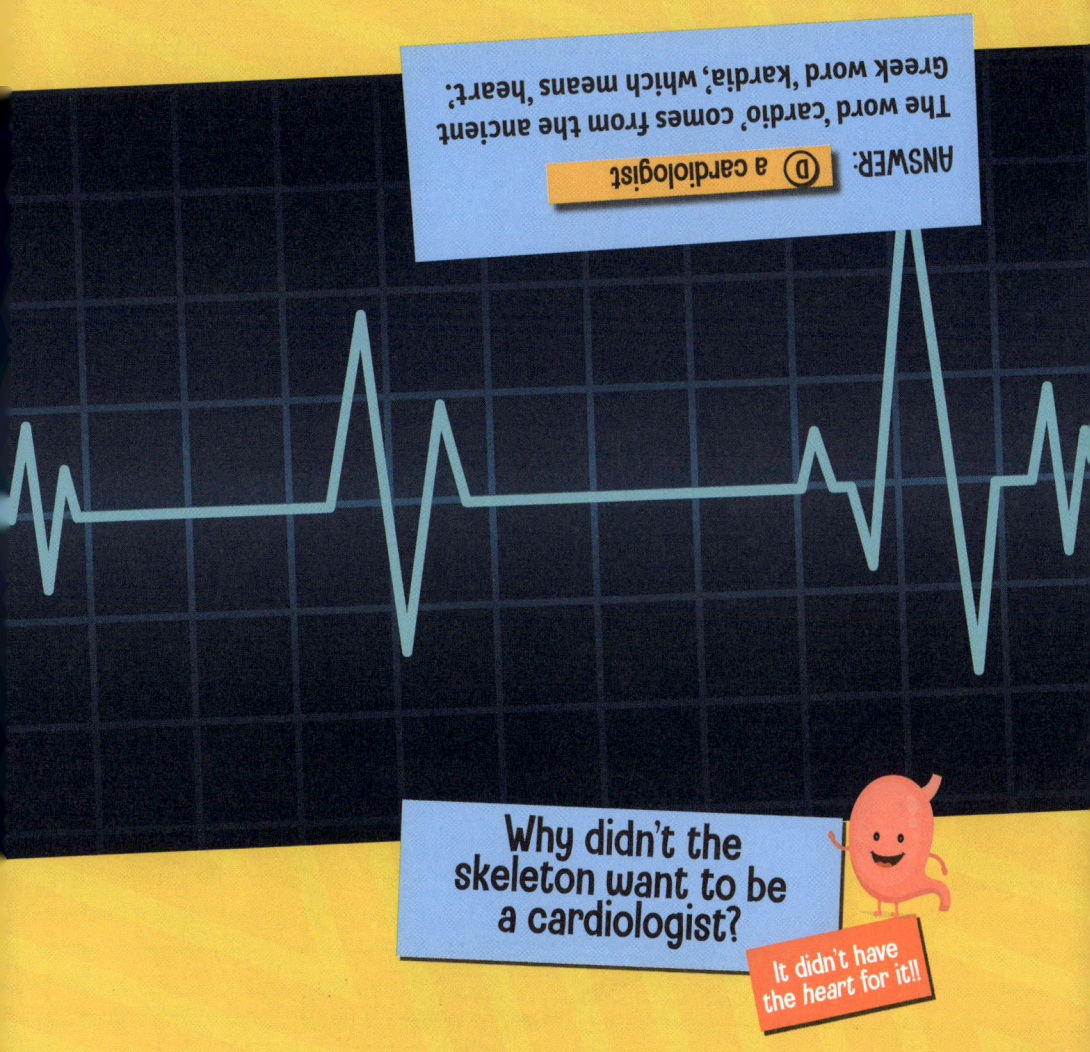

Why didn't the skeleton want to be a cardiologist?

It didn't have the heart for it!!

What instrument is used to listen to your heartbeat?

ANSWER: A stethoscope.

A stethoscope is made of a flat disc connected by a tube to two earpieces. The flat disc is placed on the patient's body and the earpieces are placed in the doctor's ears. The disc and the tube amplify the sound of a patient's lungs and heart. This means that the sounds are made louder, allowing the doctor to listen to them clearly.

Did You Know?

During an average lifetime, the human heart will beat more than 2.5 billion times!

Which device can be placed inside the body to regulate the heartbeat?

- **A** an oximeter
- **B** a pacemaker
- **C** a stethoscope
- **D** a thermometer

ANSWER: **B) a pacemaker**

A pacemaker is a small electrical device that is implanted in the body to help regulate the heartbeat. Pacemakers have helped many heart patients live longer lives.

TRUE or FALSE?

Your hair and nails are made of the same material.

ANSWER: True!

Your hair and nails are made of a tough protein called keratin. Keratin is also found in bird feathers, and hooves and horns of some animals.

Where does a sheep get a haircut?

At the baa-baa shop!

Which of these characteristics is NOT passed on from your parents?

A your height

B the shape of your lips

C the colour of your hair

D the length of your hair

Turn the page for the answer!

125

ANSWER: D

the length of your hair

Children inherit characteristics such as height, lip shape and hair colour from their parents. Length of hair is not an inherited characteristic as hair can be grown or cut to change its length.

What do you call a haircut that you get on a hill?

A cut above the rest!

Did You Know?
Our hair grows about 1 to 1.5 centimetres each month.

TRUE or FALSE?

Boys reach puberty before girls.

ANSWER: False!

Puberty is the time when a child's body starts to develop towards becoming an adult. Puberty causes physical changes and is different for boys and girls. Girls usually reach puberty before boys. Puberty starts between ages 8 and 13 in girls and ages 9 and 15 in boys.

Which part of the female reproductive system produces eggs?

- **A** the cervix
- **B** the uterus
- **C** the ovaries
- **D** the fallopian tubes

ovary

Turn the page for the answer!

130

female reproductive system

- fallopian tubes
- uterus
- ovary
- cervix

ANSWER: C

the ovaries

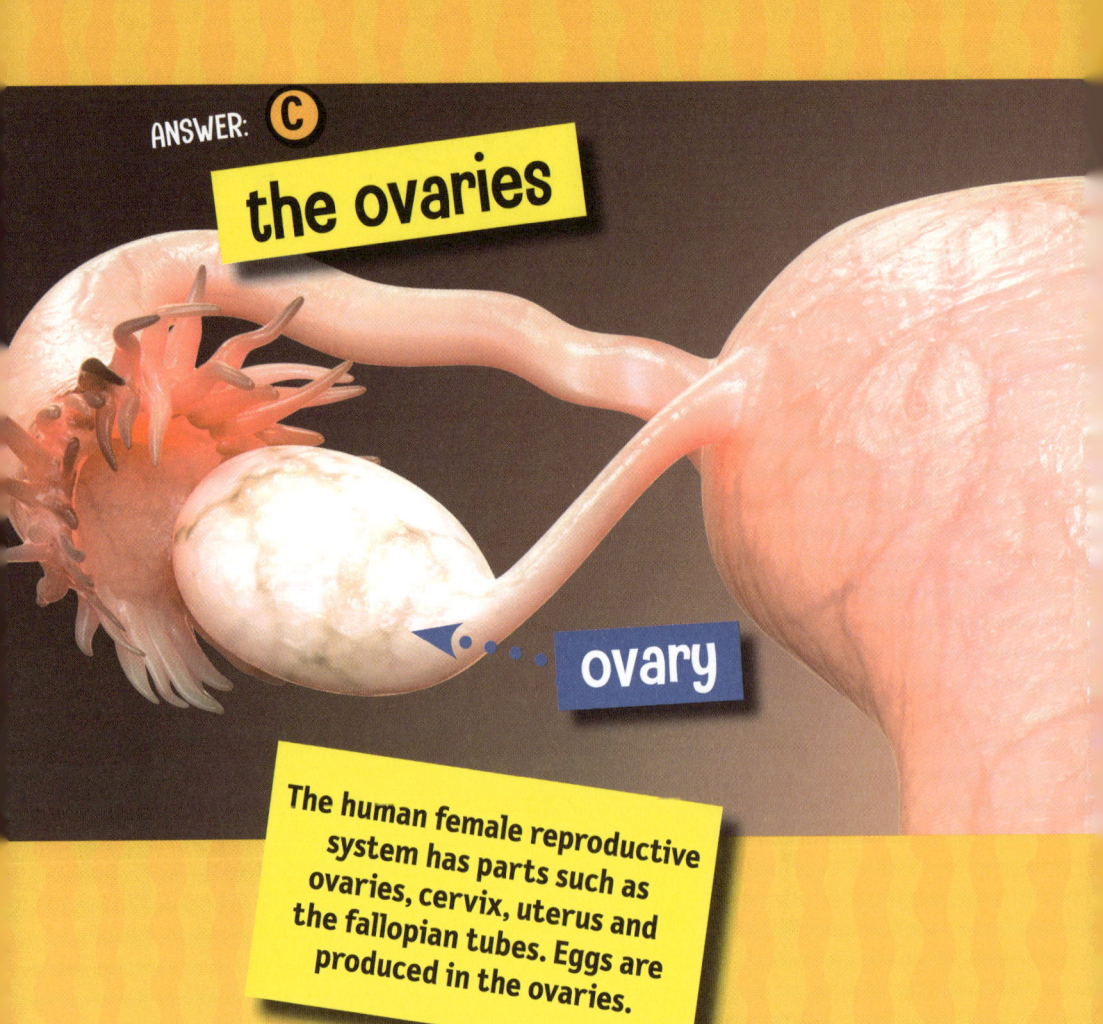

ovary

The human female reproductive system has parts such as ovaries, cervix, uterus and the fallopian tubes. Eggs are produced in the ovaries.

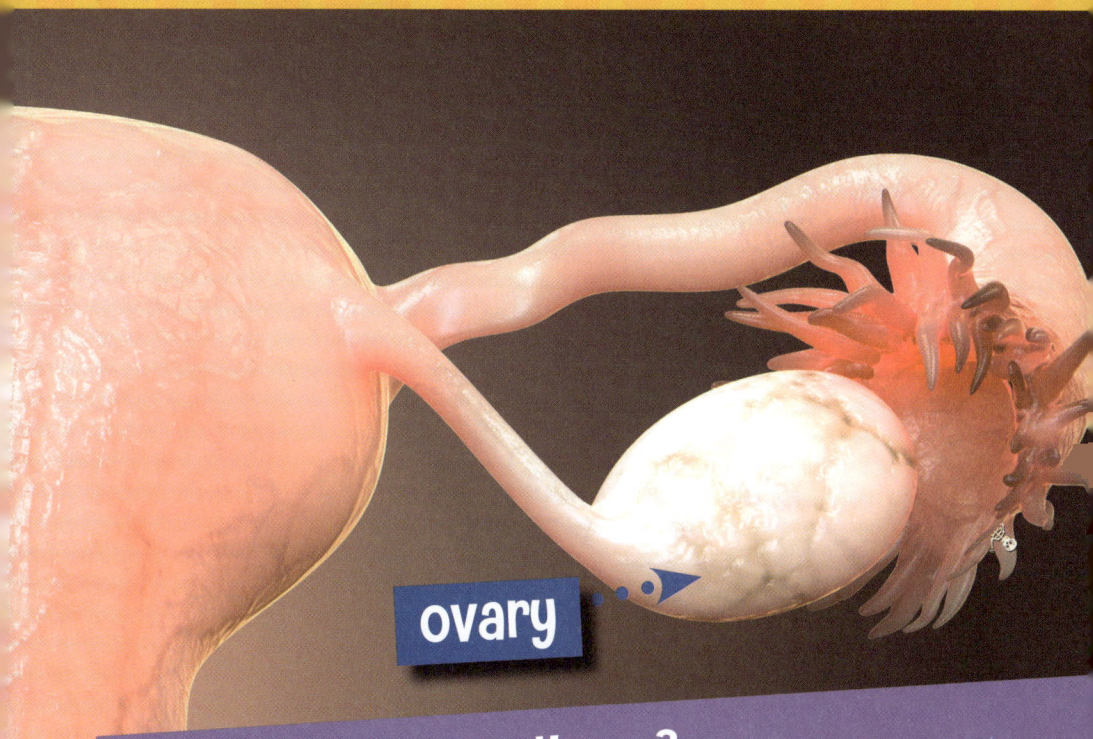

ovary

Did You Know?
Female babies are born with 1–2 million eggs in their ovaries. However, many eggs die each month so their number reduces with the person's age. The eggs mature at puberty. A female typically has around 300,000 to 500,000 eggs remaining when puberty begins.

How many sperms does it take to fertilise a human egg?

ANSWER: One!

Fertilisation is the process by which an egg and a sperm fuse. This leads to the formation of an embryo, which may develop into a baby. During fertilisation, many sperms surround the egg, but only one of them fuses with the egg. Sperms are made by the male reproductive system.

134

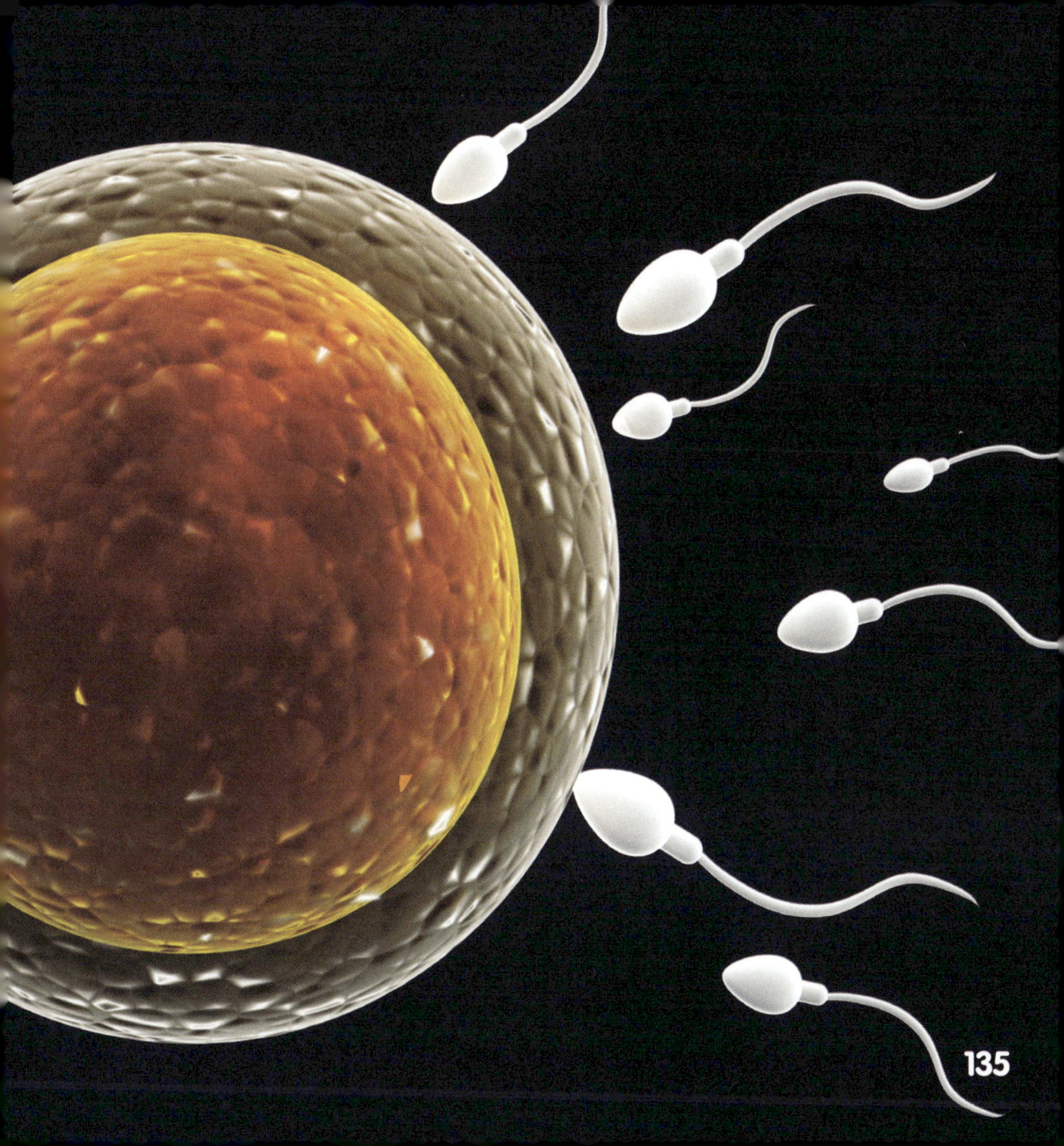

How long does it take for a human baby to develop inside the mother's womb?

- **A** 3 months
- **B** 6 months
- **C** 9 months
- **D** 1 year

How does an embryo get its food?

Womb service!

ANSWER: C) 9 months

A human baby usually spends about nine months developing in the mother's womb. A womb is an organ of the female reproductive system. It is also called a uterus.

137

How does a developing baby receive oxygen and nutrients in the womb?

umbilical cord

ANSWER: Through the umbilical cord.

A developing baby is connected to the mother's body by a tube called the umbilical cord. The baby receives oxygen and nutrients from the mother's blood through the umbilical cord.

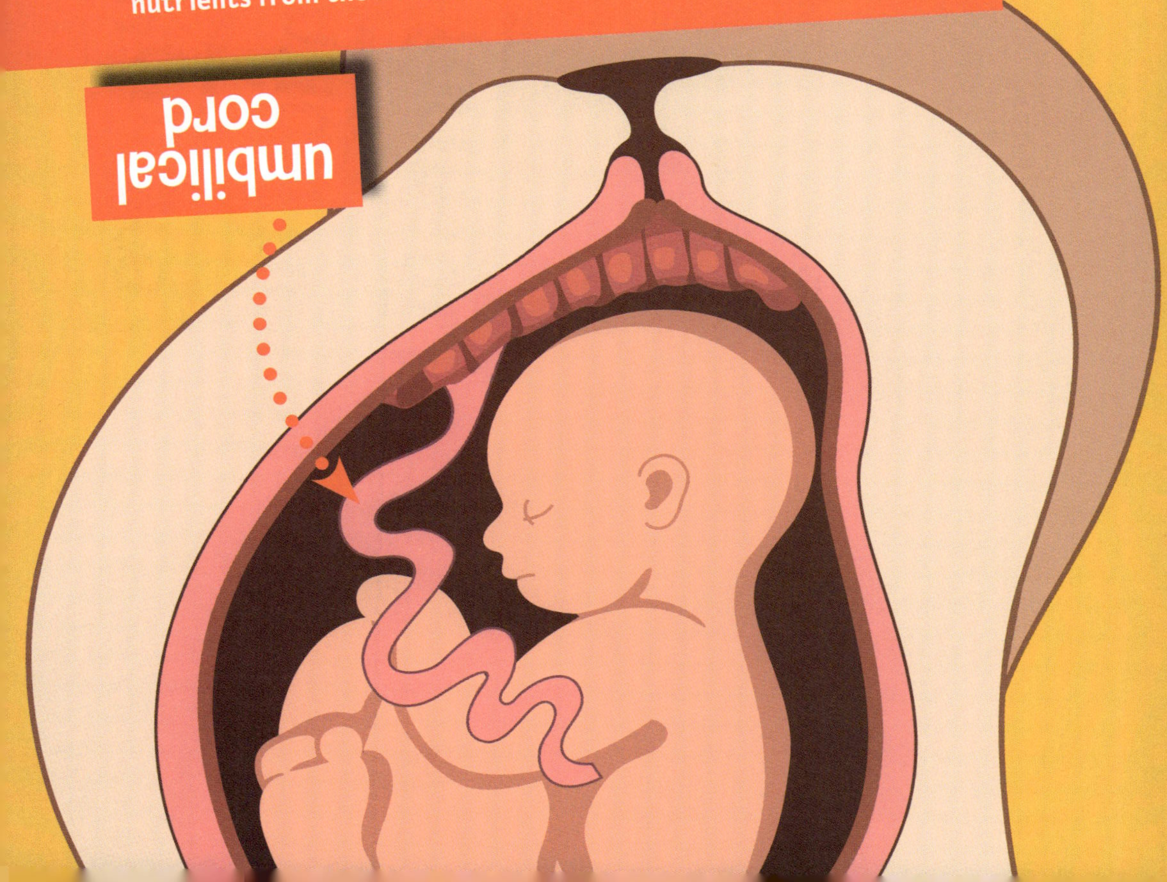

How are identical twins formed?

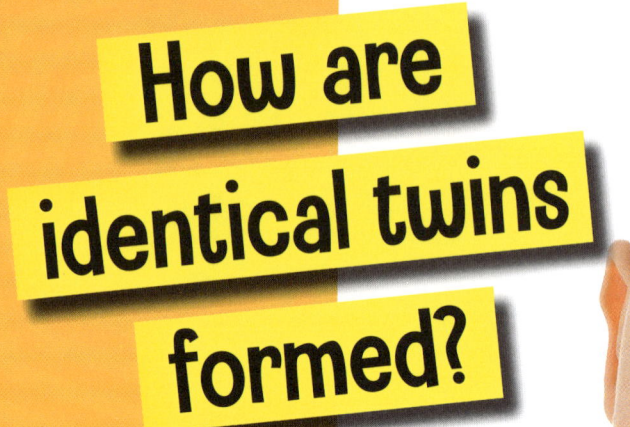

- **A** when 2 sperms fertilise 1 egg
- **B** when 1 sperm fertilises 2 eggs
- **C** when 2 sperms fertilise 2 eggs
- **D** when 1 fertilised egg divides into 2

Turn the page for the answer!

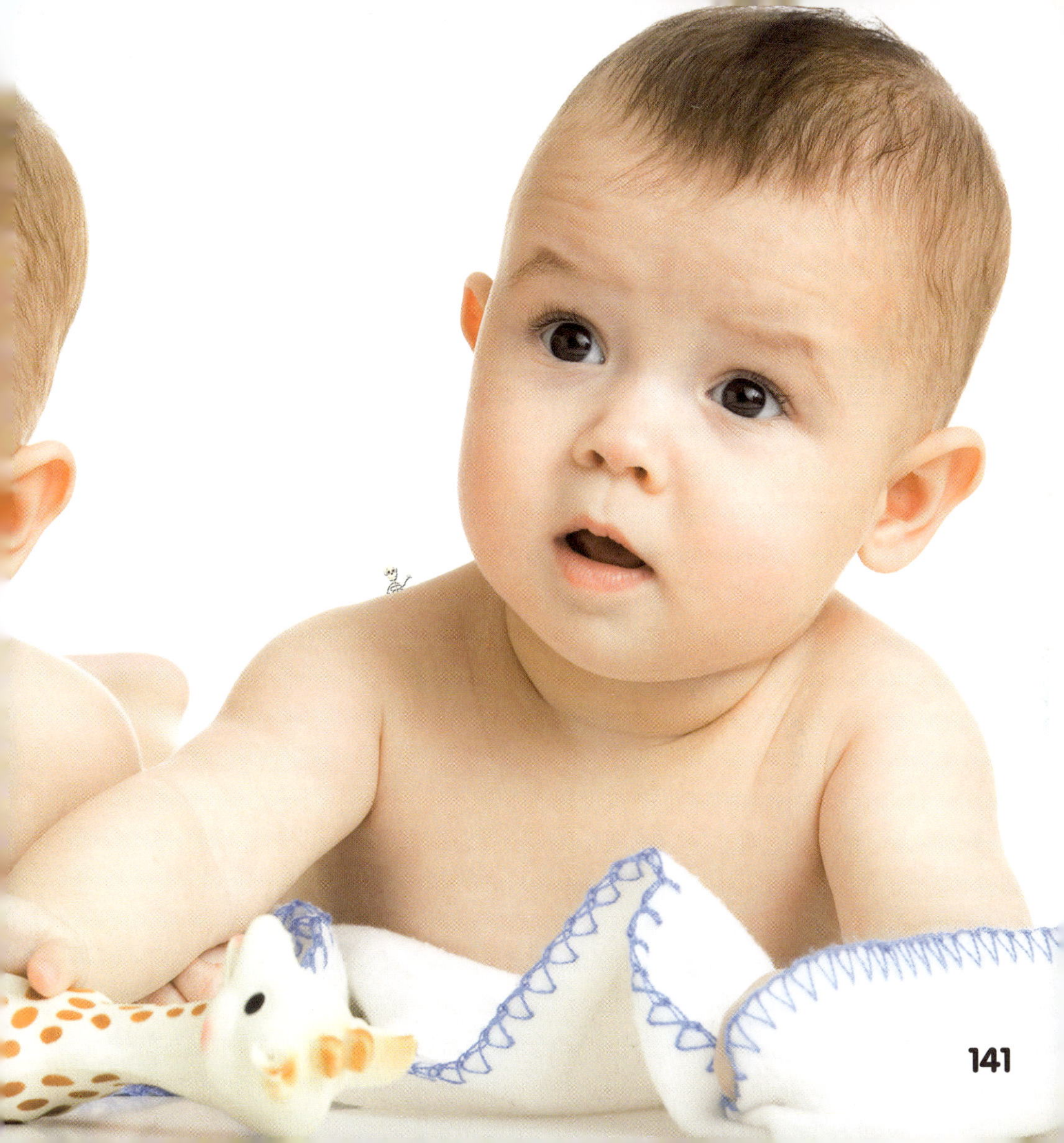

ANSWER: **D**

when 1 fertilised egg divides into 2

The two resulting eggs develop into two babies. The babies are of the same gender and are identical.

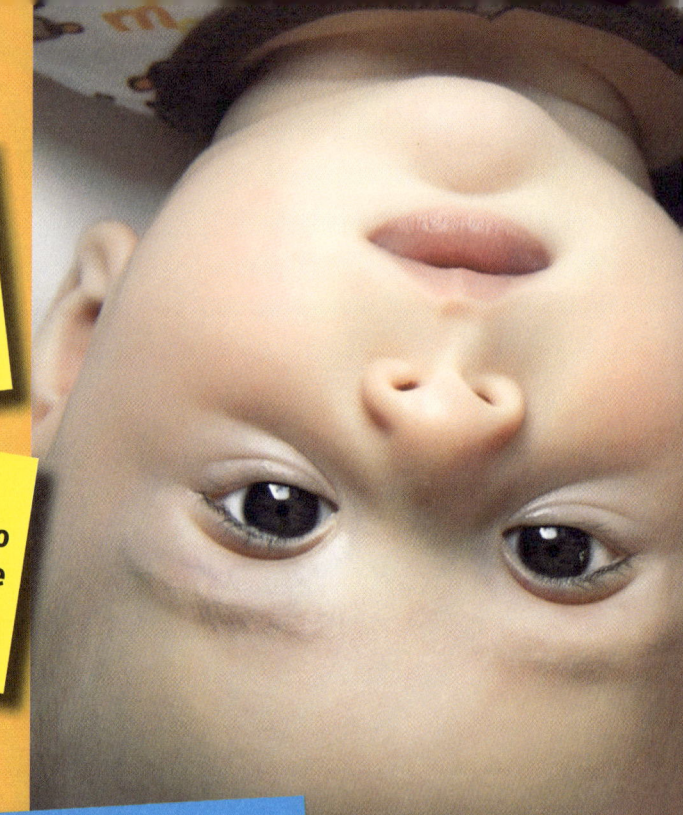

Did You Know?

Twins may also result from two eggs being fertilised by two sperms. Such twins are not identical and are known as fraternal twins. Fraternal twins can be of different genders.

Kate had an identical twin. What was her name?

Dupli-Kate!

143

Which of the following shows how a body system is formed?

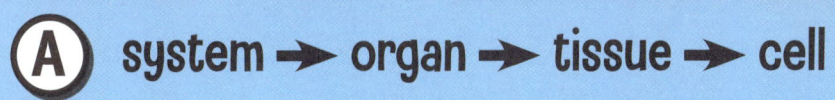

- (A) system → organ → tissue → cell
- (B) organ → tissue → cell → system
- (C) cell → tissue → organ → system
- (D) tissue → cell → organ → system

Turn the page for the answer!

145

ANSWER: **C**

cell → tissue → organ → system

Cells make up tissues, tissues make up organs, and organs make up systems. Cells are the smallest units of life. Cells of a certain type group together to form tissue. An organ is formed when different types of tissues work together to perform a function. Various organs work together to form an organ system such as the digestive system.

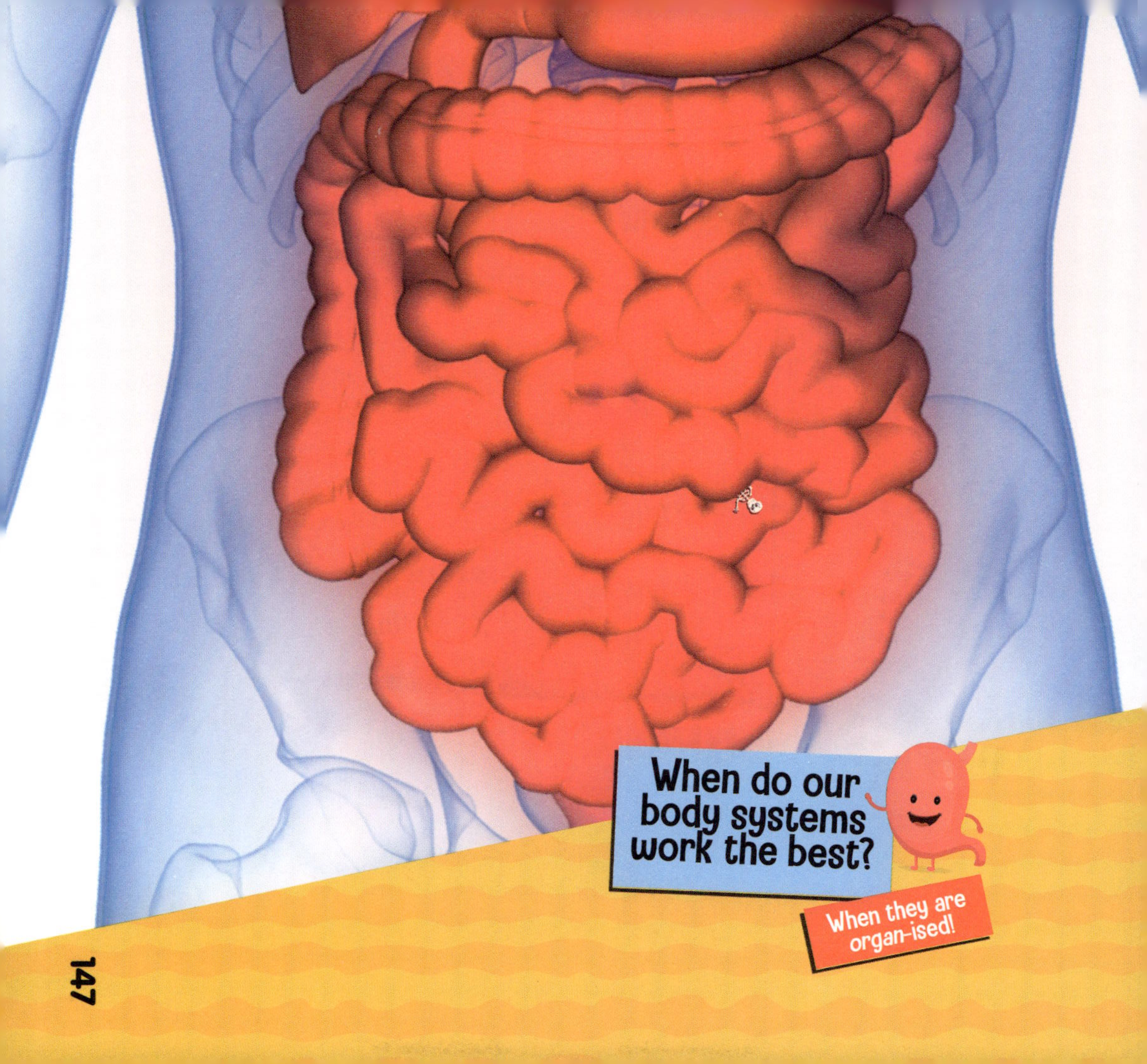

When do our body systems work the best?

When they are organ-ised!

147

How many cells are in your body?

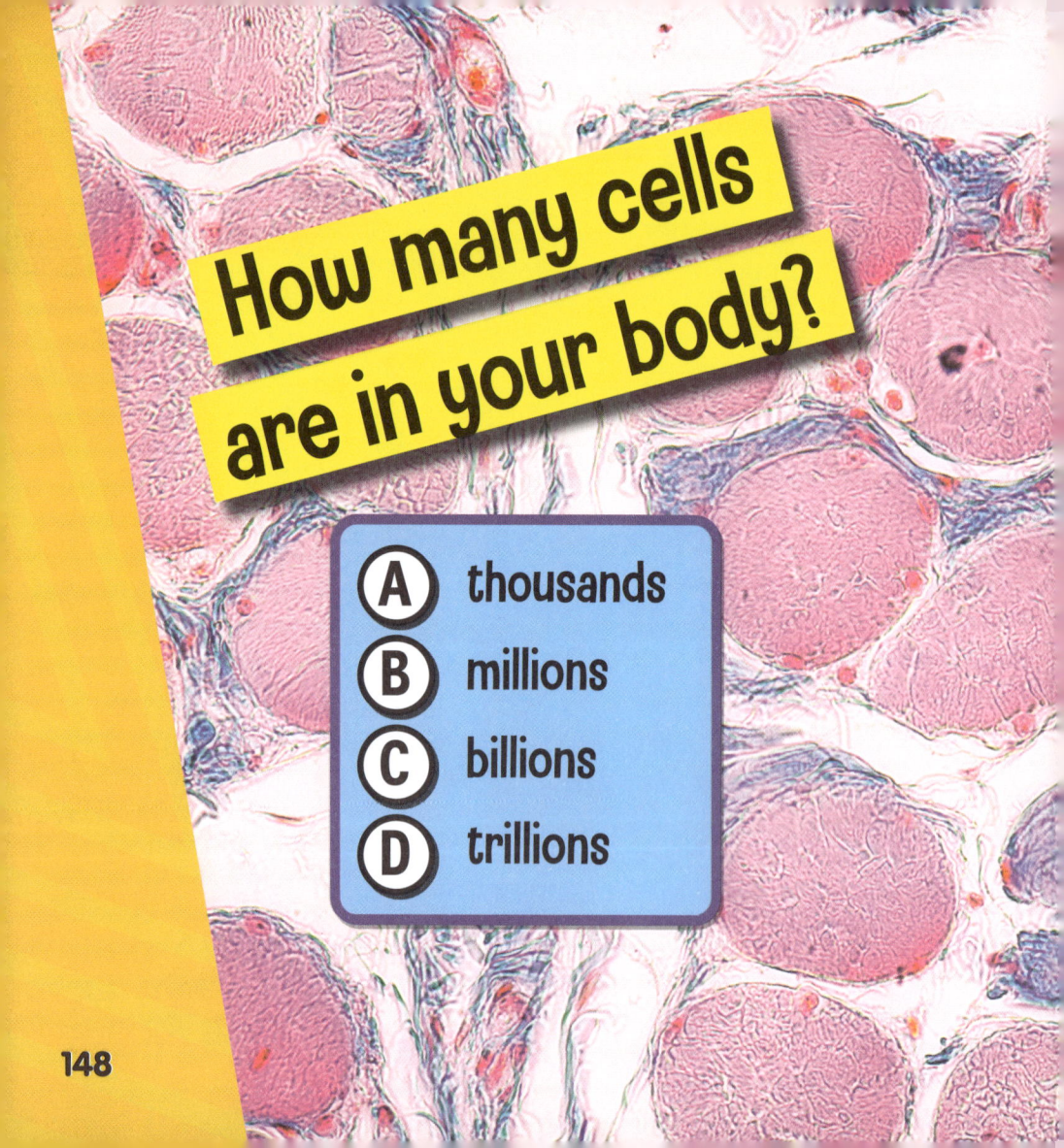

- **A** thousands
- **B** millions
- **C** billions
- **D** trillions

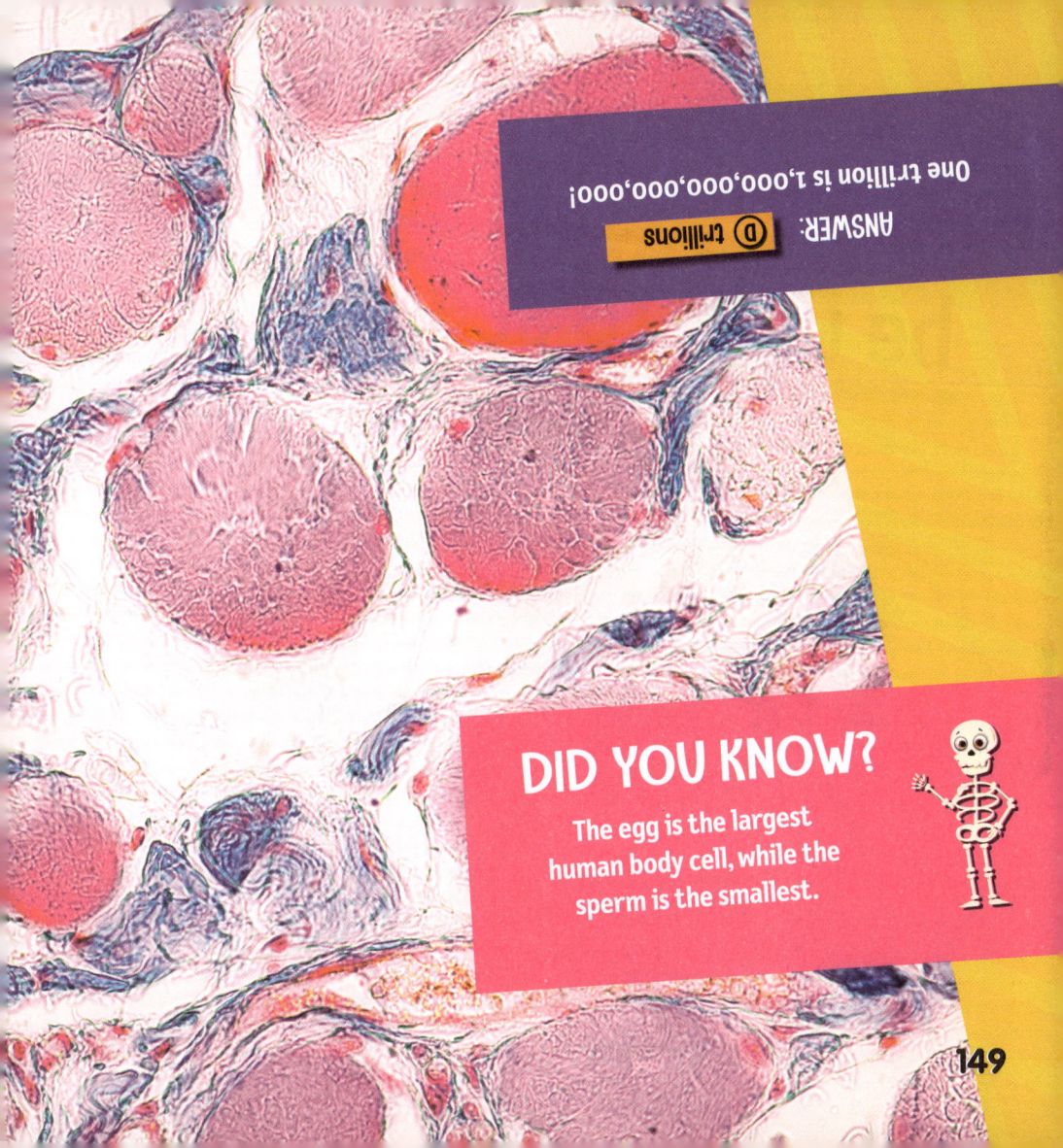

ANSWER: D) trillions
One trillion is 1,000,000,000,000!

DID YOU KNOW?

The egg is the largest human body cell, while the sperm is the smallest.

Which instrument can be used to see cells?

telescope

periscope

150

stethoscope

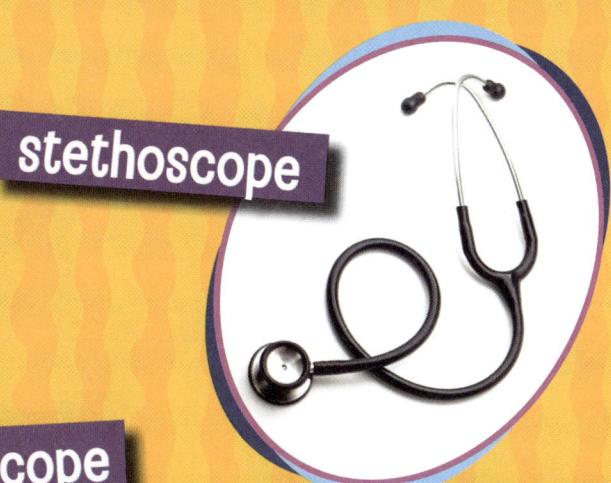

microscope

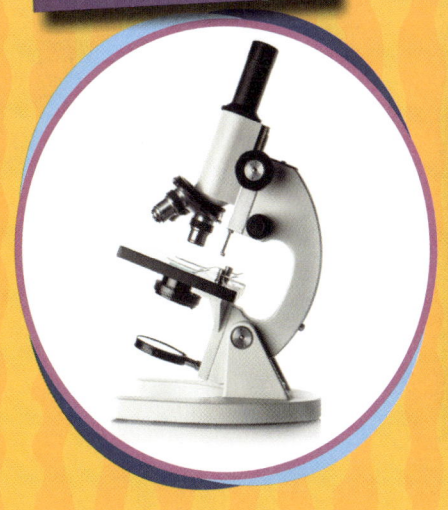

- **A** a telescope
- **B** a periscope
- **C** a microscope
- **D** a stethoscope

Turn the page for the answer!

151

ANSWER: **C**

a microscope

Cells are too small to be seen with our naked eyes. We need instruments called microscopes to see them. Microscopes make things appear much bigger than they are.

DID YOU KNOW?

Modern microscopes are very powerful and can take detailed photographs of tiny things such as pollen grains and fleas.

What kind of pictures can you take with a microscope?

Cell-fies!

Which part of a cell controls everything that happens inside the cell?

ANSWER: The nucleus.

The nucleus is known as the 'brain of the cell.' Just like how your brain controls all the parts of the body, the nucleus controls all activities of the cell.

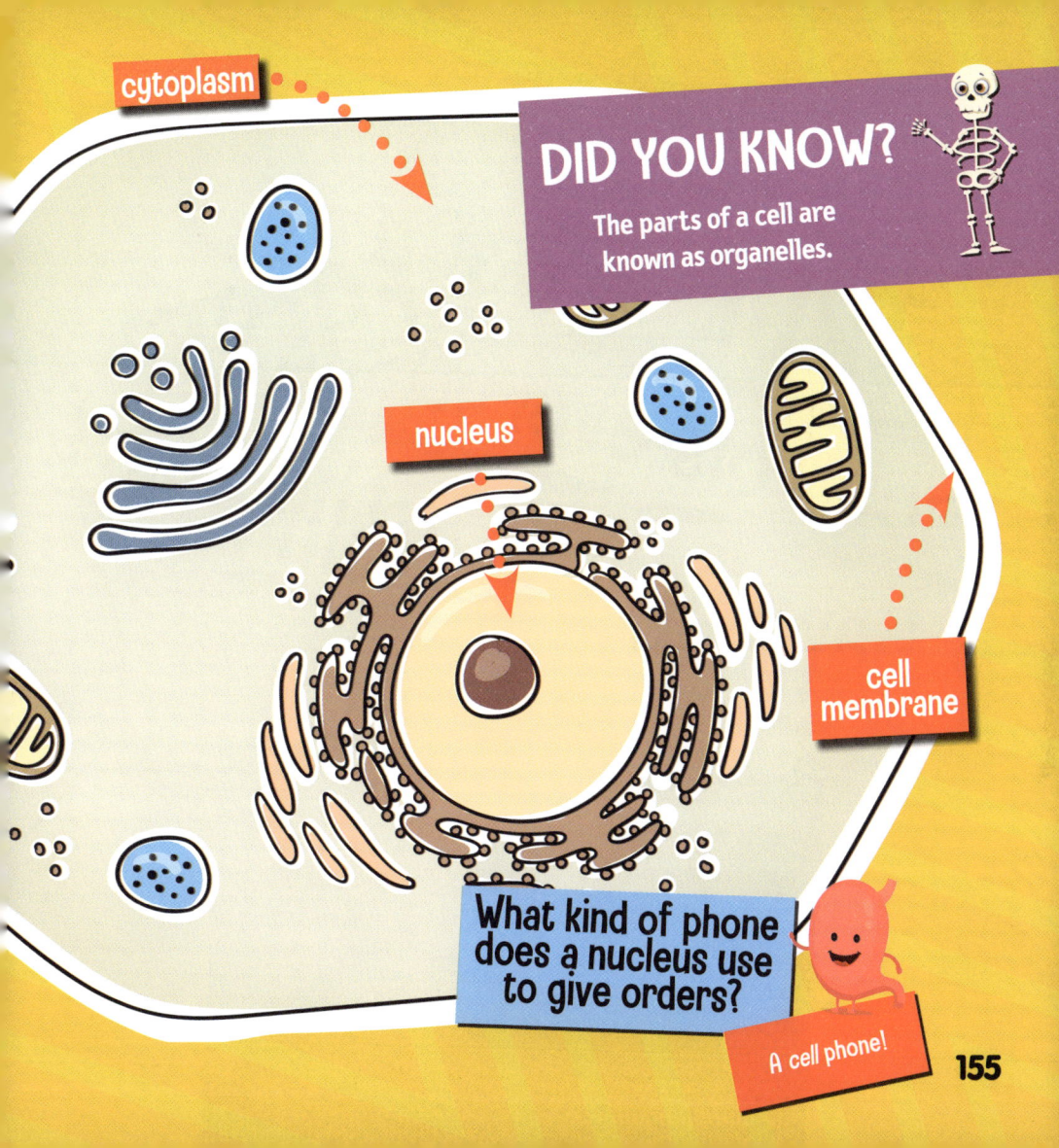

cytoplasm

DID YOU KNOW?
The parts of a cell are known as organelles.

nucleus

cell membrane

What kind of phone does a nucleus use to give orders?

A cell phone!

155

TRUE or FALSE?

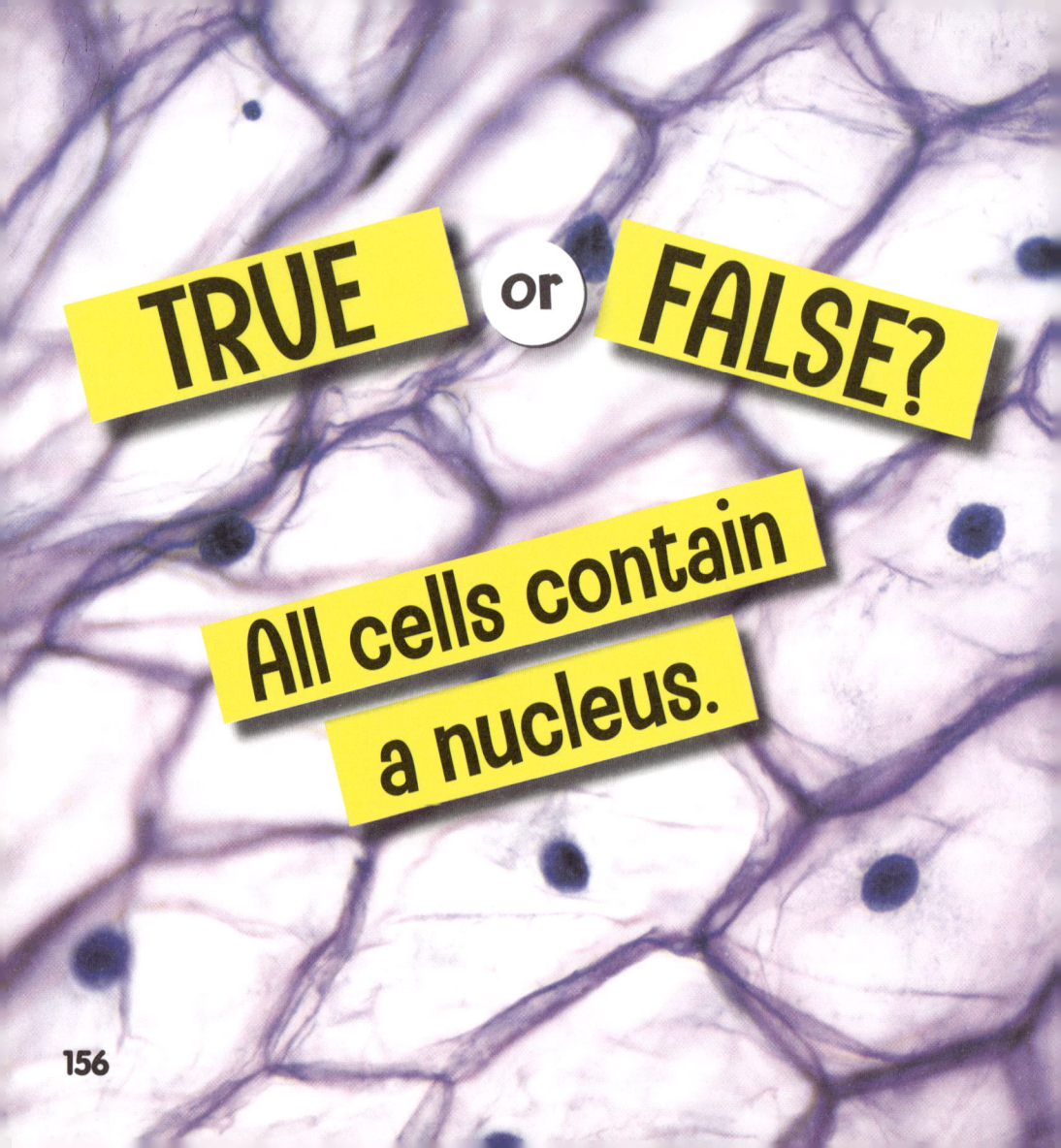

All cells contain a nucleus.

ANSWER:
False!

Not all cells contain a nucleus. Cells such as red blood cells do not contain a nucleus. The main function of red blood cells is to carry oxygen. The absence of the nucleus in red blood cells creates more space for the oxygen-carrying protein called haemoglobin. This makes the red blood cells more efficient in their function.

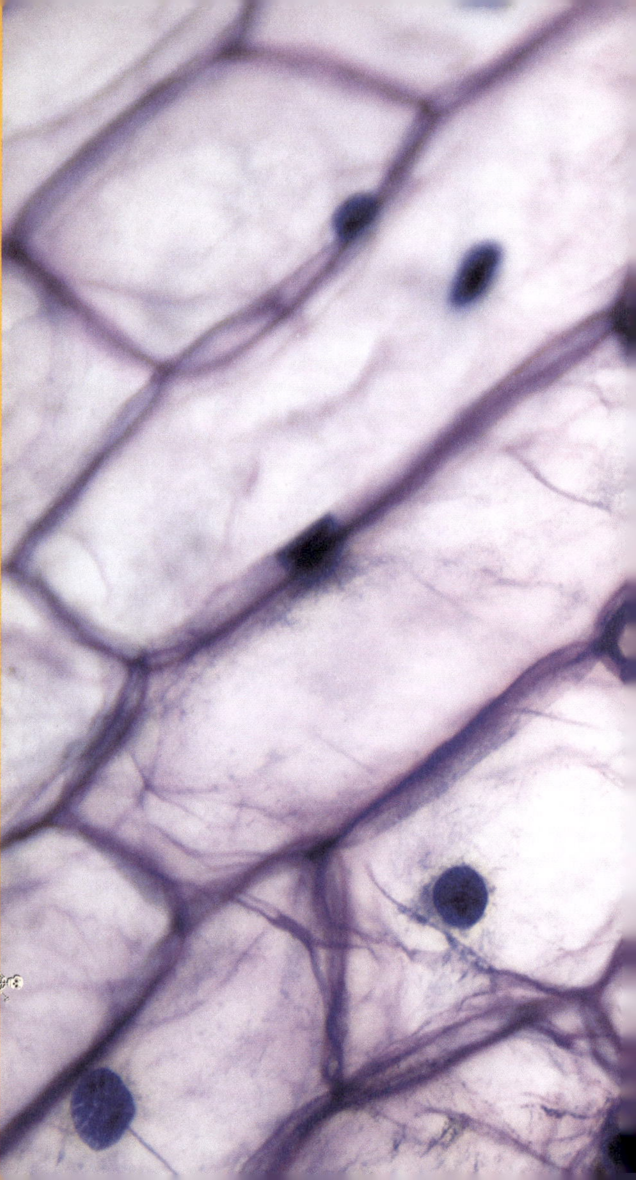

Which of these parts is found in a plant cell but NOT in an animal cell?

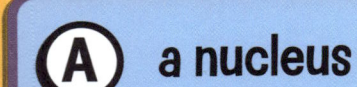

A. a nucleus
B. a cell wall
C. cytoplasm
D. a cell membrane

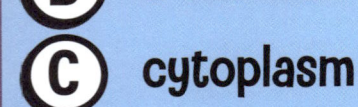

158

ANSWER: Ⓑ a cell wall

Plants need a rigid structure to help them grow upright and protect themselves from injury. The cell wall helps to provide that. Animals do not need cell walls. They have a skeleton for support. They also need to have flexible bodies to move about to find food and escape danger.

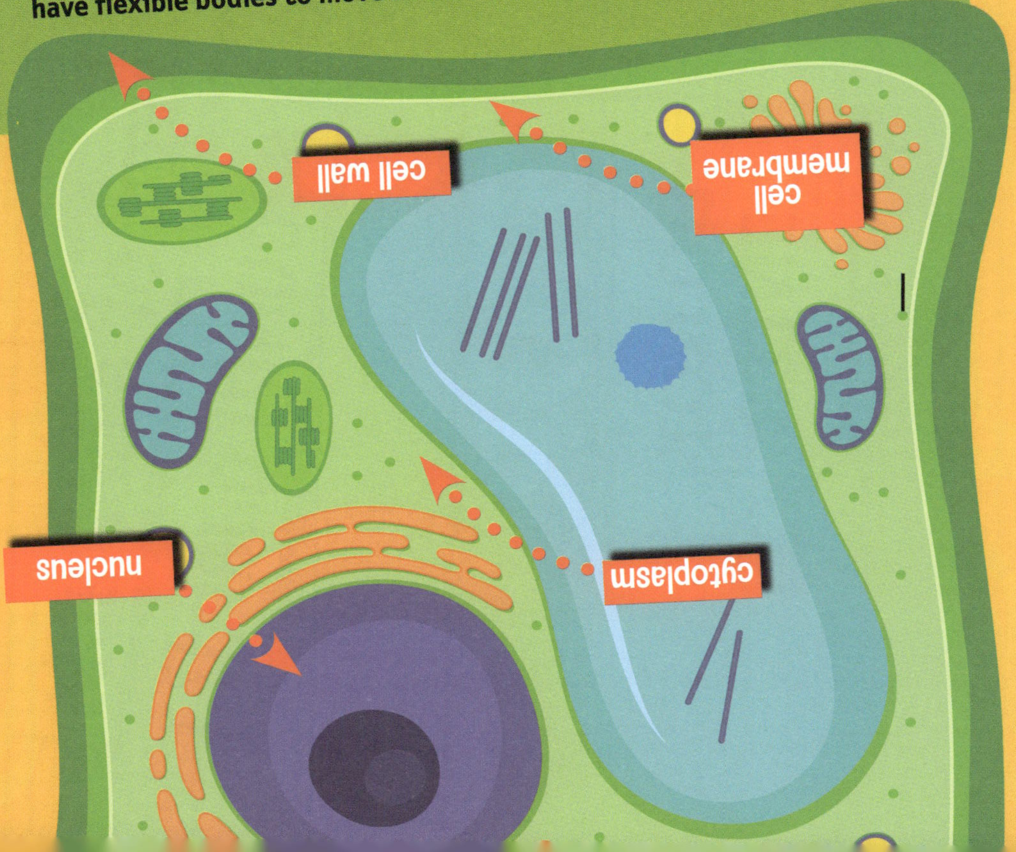

- nucleus
- cell wall
- cytoplasm
- cell membrane

What part of a cell acts like a security guard?

ANSWER: The cell membrane.

The cell membrane is a thin layer surrounding the cell. It controls the movement of substances into and out of the cell.

cytoplasm

nucleus

cell membrane

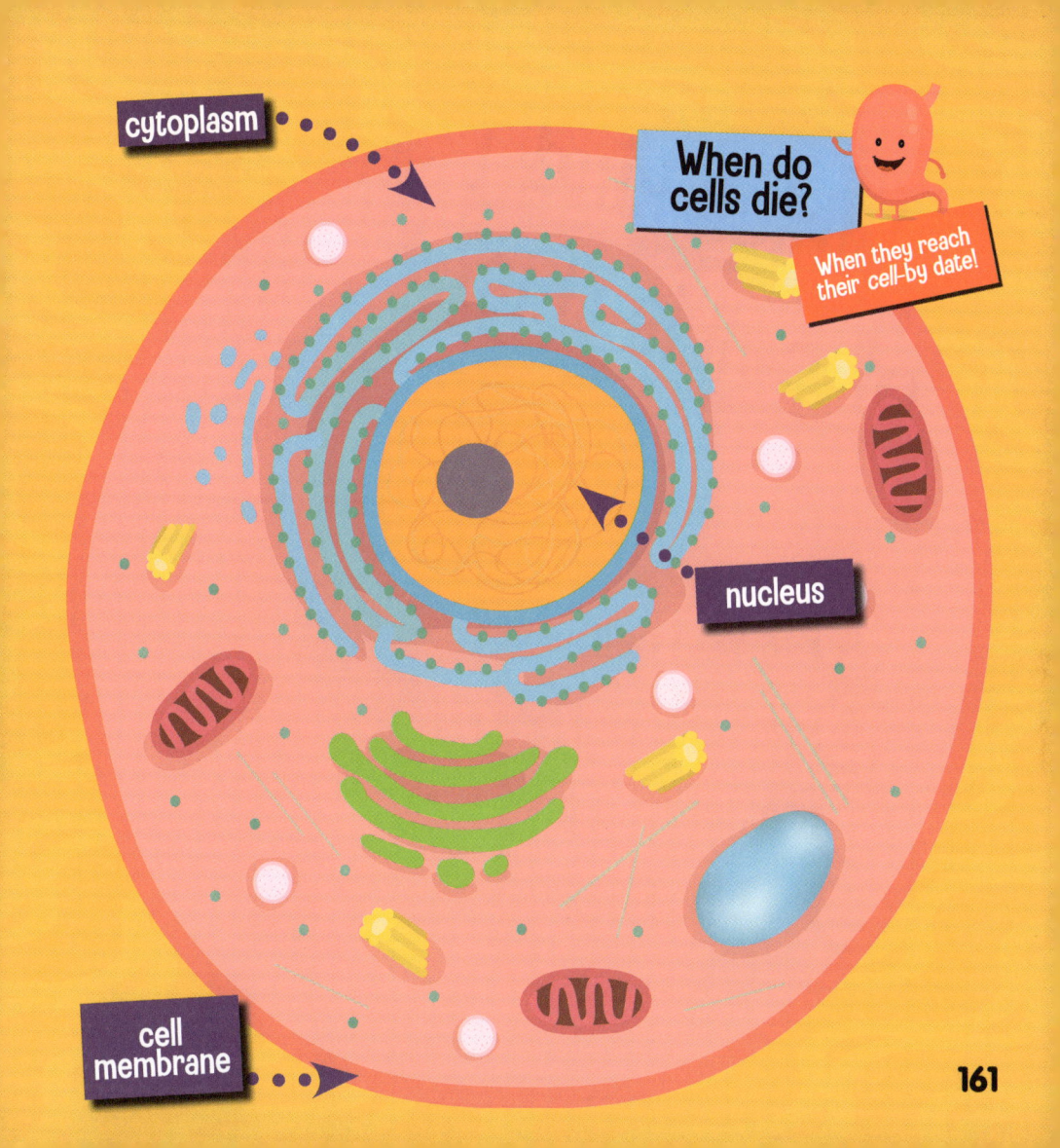

When do cells die?

When they reach their cell-by date!

Which kind of cell is this?

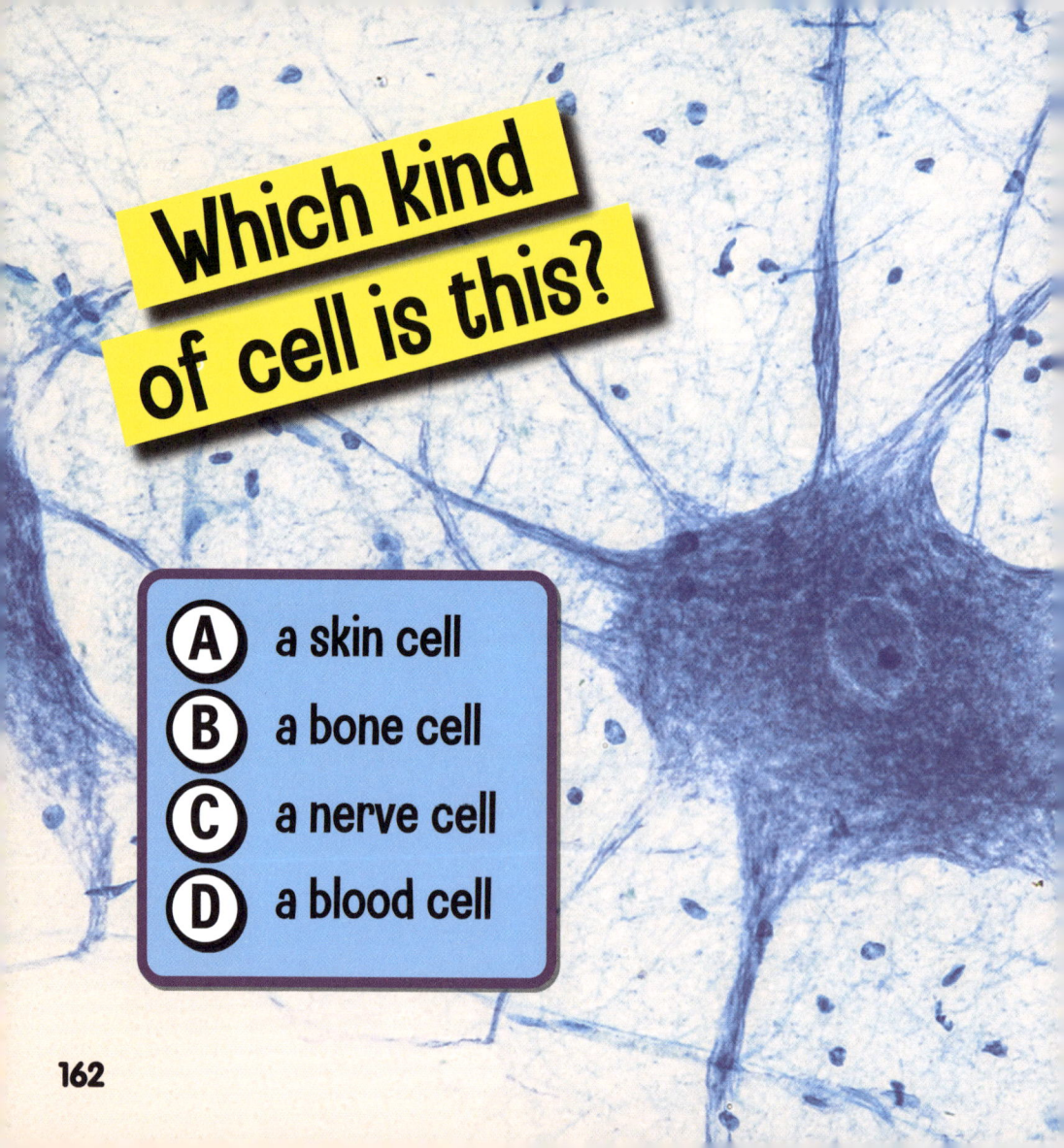

- **A** a skin cell
- **B** a bone cell
- **C** a nerve cell
- **D** a blood cell

ANSWER:
C) a nerve cell

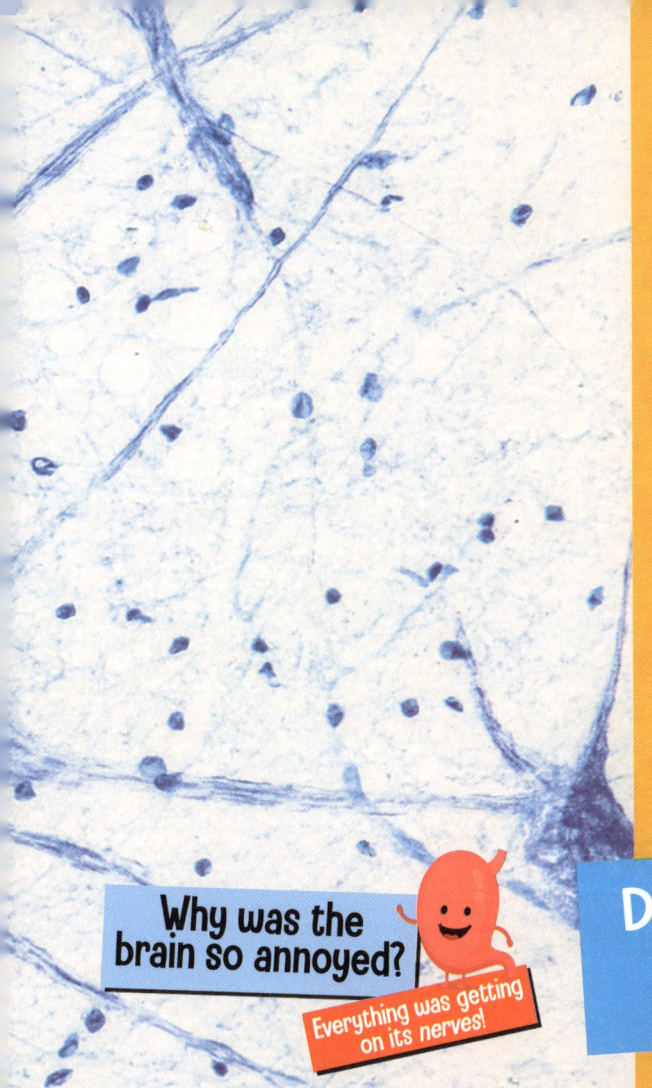

Your nervous system is made up of the brain, the spinal cord, and a complex network of nerves. The nervous system uses cells called nerve cells (also known as neurons) to send messages back and forth between the brain and the different parts of the body.

Why was the brain so annoyed?
Everything was getting on its nerves!

Did You Know?
The brain has billions of nerve cells!

163

Which disease is associated with abnormal cells in the body?

- **A** cancer
- **B** dengue
- **C** measles
- **D** influenza

ANSWER: Ⓐ cancer

Cancer occurs when cells in a part of the body start to increase in number in an uncontrolled manner. Cancer is a deadly disease, killing millions of people worldwide each year. There are more than 100 types of cancer.

165

Bonus Quiz Time!

Match the keywords to their definitions.

___ Blood
___ Cell
___ Circulatory system
___ Digestive system
___ Heart
___ Lungs
___ Muscular system
___ Reproductive system
___ Respiratory system
___ Skeletal system

1. The smallest unit of life
2. The organ system that breaks down food into simple substances and absorbs them
3. The organ system made up of muscles
4. The organ system that helps the body to take in oxygen and remove carbon dioxide
5. The organ system made up of bones
6. Organs that help the body to exchange gases with the surroundings
7. The organ system that transports substances to different parts of the body
8. A liquid that transports substances around the body
9. A muscular organ that pumps blood throughout the body
10. The organ system that allows living things to produce young

Answers

BONUS QUIZ ANSWERS: Blood - 8; Cell - 1; Circulatory system - 7; Digestive system - 2; Heart - 9; Lungs - 6; Muscular syetm - 3; Reproductive system - 10; Respiratory system - 4; Skeletal system - 5.

Which pages was Skip Skeleton hiding on?

Pages 17, 18, 27, 38, 41, 49, 53, 62, 64, 69, 74, 82, 86, 100, 103, 111, 121, 123, 127, 133, 141, 147, 153, 157 and 165.

167

Finished reading the book?

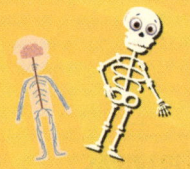

Follow these steps to get your own *Quiz Champs* certificate!

1. Solve the crossword puzzle using the given clues.
2. Identify the letters on the boxes with Skip Skeleton ( ).
3. Unscramble the letters to form a word. That's your password!
4. Enter the password in the PDF file on www.tinyurl.com/quizchampscert to download your *Quiz Champs* certificate!

168

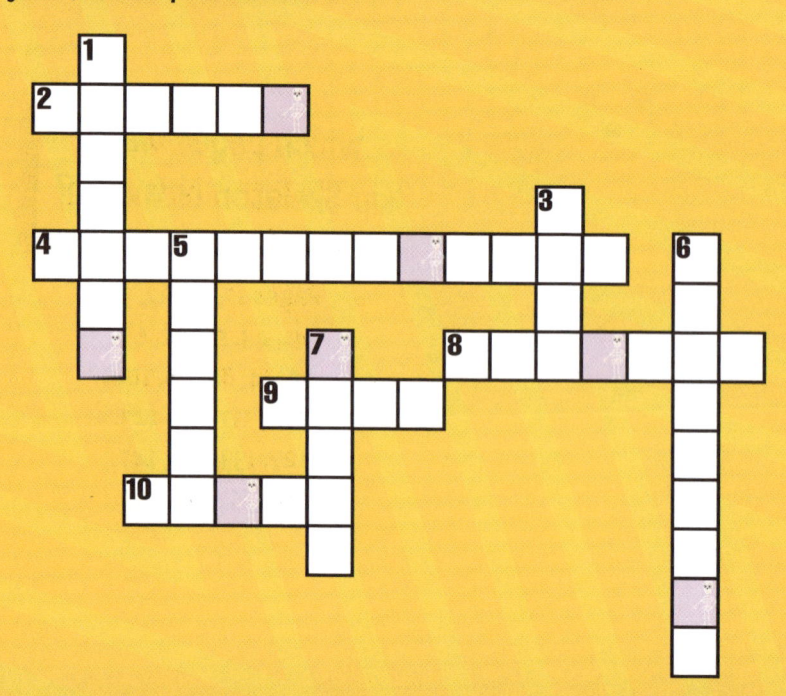

ACROSS

2. A tube that joins the mouth to the stomach
4. The fusing of an egg and a sperm
8. The part of the skeletal system that protects the heart
9. The smallest unit of life
10. The longest bone in the human body

DOWN

1. The 'brain' of a cell
3. The part of the mother's body where an unborn baby develops
5. A sense organ that helps us taste
6. The process that breaks down food into simpler substances
7. The organ that pumps blood around the body

I have identified the letters: __ __ __ __ __ __ __

I have unscrambled them to form my password! __ __ __ __ __ __ __

Quiz Champs

The *Quiz Champs* series has been specially crafted to be a fun and educational learning experience for young learners. The series is aligned with the Singapore primary Science syllabus and the Cambridge primary Science curriculum, and also includes enrichment questions to stretch curious minds. Answers and additional information have been provided to aid in learning, revision and preparation for testing.

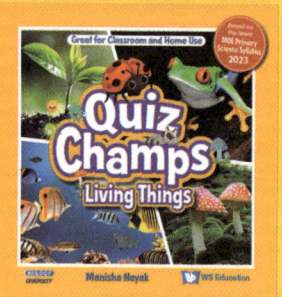

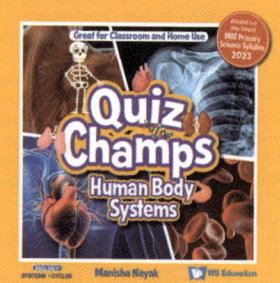

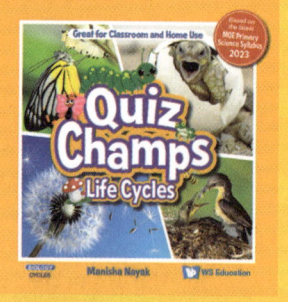

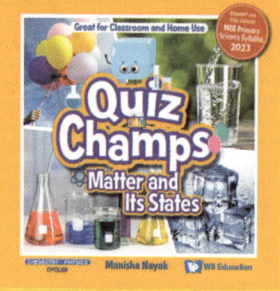

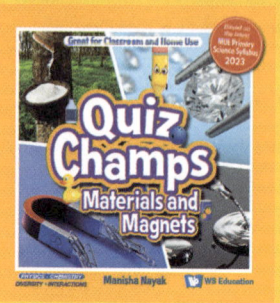

- Quiz Champs: Living Things
- Quiz Champs: Human Body Systems
- Quiz Champs: Life Cycles
- Quiz Champs: Matter and Its States
- Quiz Champs: Materials and Magnets

I'M A FUTURE SCIENTIST!

The *I'm a Future Scientist!* series is based on the Science Centre Singapore's longstanding and highly popular Young Scientist badge programme. This exciting series of full-colour books for 6–12-year-olds will spark sustained interest in scientific fields, such as botany, zoology, marine biology, conservation and the environment, astronomy, and many more, while delivering primary-school-level Science learning points in an engaging and relatable way!

Through clearly written educational articles, fun cartoons, suggested hands-on activities, as well as full-colour photographs and illustrations, these books are the perfect companions for budding scientists to delve further into a wide range of fields of Science.

In addition, Augmented Reality (AR) elements will also help to bring Science alive for children, helping them to retain the information provided better, and inspiring better learning! And, as a bonus, earn points for the Young Scientist Badge programme from Science Centre Singapore, using the links inside!

World of Science

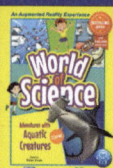

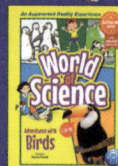

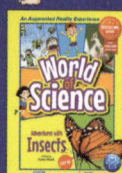

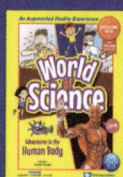

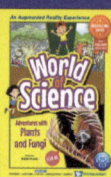

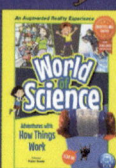

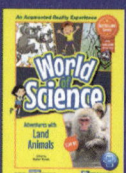

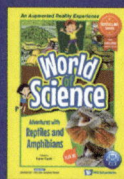

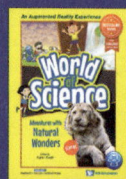

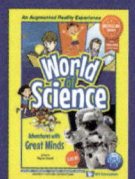

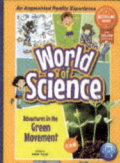

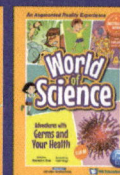

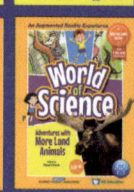

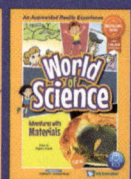

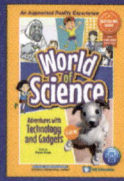

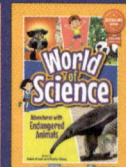

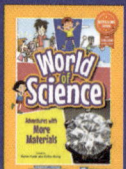

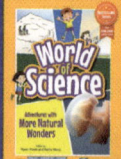

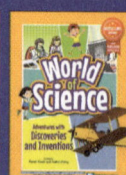

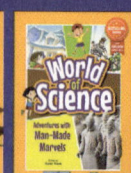

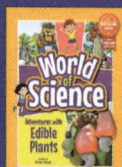

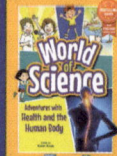

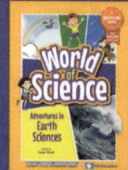

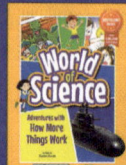

BESTSELLING Series — OVER 100,000 COPIES SOLD

- Adventures with Aquatic Creatures
- Adventures with Birds
- Adventures with Insects
- Adventures in the Human Body
- Adventures with Plants and Fungi
- Adventures with How Things Work
- Adventures with Land Animals
- Adventures with Reptiles and Amphibians
- Adventures with Natural Wonders
- Adventures with Great Minds
- Adventures in the Green Movement
- Adventures with Germs and Your Health
- Adventures with More Land Animals
- Adventures with Materials
- Adventures with Technology and Gadgets
- Adventures with Endangered Animals
- Adventures with More Materials
- Adventures with More Natural Wonders
- Adventures with Useful Plants and Fungi
- Adventures with Discoveries and Inventions
- Adventures with Man-Made Marvels
- Adventures with Edible Plants
- Adventures with Health and the Human Body
- Adventures in Earth Sciences
- Adventures with How More Things Work
- Gutsy Guts Adventures
- The Worldwide Adventures of Biogirl MJ

To receive updates about children's titles from WS Education, go to https://www.worldscientific.com/page/newsletter/subscribe, choose "Education", click on "Children's Books" and key in your email address.

Follow us for our latest releases, videos and promotions:

@worldscientificedu (Instagram)
@worldscientificedu (YouTube)

WS Education